WINGNUTS

WINGNUTS

How the Lunatic Fringe
Is Hijacking America

JOHN AVLON

New York

Published by Beast Books.
Beast Books is a co-publishing venture with the Perseus Books Group.

Editorial production by *Marra*thon Production Services,
www.marrathon.net

DESIGN BY JANE RAESE
Text set in 12-point Apollo

Cataloging-in-Publication Data for this book is available from the
Library of Congress.

ISBN 978-0-9842951-1-1

10 9 8 7 6 5 4 3 2 1

For Margaret

CONTENTS

FOREWORD

by Tina Brown, Editor-in-Chief of The Daily Beast

Wingnuts is the first book bearing the imprint of Beast Books. Twelve months into our online operations at The Daily Beast, we felt it was time to take advantage of digital technology and provide a new outlet for writers who have something relevant to say that cannot wait for the snail's pace of traditional publishing schedules.

Beast Books will be longer than conventional long-form magazine articles but shorter than conventional nonfiction books. They will be published digitally and distributed on multiple platforms, and will soon thereafter be available as handy paperbacks. They'll provide megabyte edification—and high-voltage provocation—with the ambition of enlarging our understanding of the complexities we chronicle every day at the fast and furious pace of breaking news on The Daily Beast.

Our political commentator John Avlon was a clear choice to kick off Beast Books. His assiduous reporting and his smart, passionate commentary have impressed colleagues and readers alike. All along, he has been keeping detailed track of America's descent into bitter partisanship despite the advent of a president who fervently hoped for a politics that would be the very opposite.

It was Avlon who broke the story of the thirty-eight-year-old Young Republican leader Audra Shay, who had laughed at a supporter's racist comments on Facebook. Shay littered her own Web site with charges that the president was "anti-American," one of the new buzzwords of what Avlon, in this book, labels the "fright wing" of the political spectrum.

"Finding her offensive reaction online was a window into the way the Internet can help trace the rise of extremism in politics," Avlon tells me. "It was almost surreal, almost funny, the way Shay was caught red-handed. Yet despite that, the Young Republicans elected her as their president! It made me realize how deep the rot had gotten." The explosion of traffic on his Shay story suggested that the incident had galvanized opinion left and right.

Avlon knows politics inside and out. Now thirty-seven, he was the youngest but longest-serving speech-writer in the administration of former Mayor Rudy Giuliani. After 9/11, he wrote the official eulogies for the many New York City firefighters, New York City police officers, Port Authority officers and other emergency workers who died that day. Though he crafted all those speeches for a Republican mayor—and was deputy policy director for Giuliani's 2008 campaign—he has a passion for what Arthur Schlesinger, Jr., called "the vital center." In a year of writing for The Daily Beast, he has punched left and (especially) right at the extremes of angry, partisan incivility that have hijacked American politics and thwarted progress.

Avlon adopted the term Wingnuts to describe the growing number of wreckers of our national debate. Discourse? That's too civilized a term for what we hear when we watch cable TV or log on to any one of the innumerable, foaming partisan Web sites—a hectoring cacophony of mistrust and ill will, usually uninformed, always vehement.

Who are the Wingnuts and what do they represent for American politics? One of Avlon's purposes in writing his book is to identify the leaders. Another is to describe the origins of randomly formed convictions that strike most of us as crazy but often have a core of justified grievance, a legitimate if lurid fear of where the country they love is headed.

To discount the Wingnuts as entirely delusional is too easy. And it's a mistake: When we are so repelled by the language that we deny a genuine point, we merely aggravate the paranoia that agitates many of the Wingnuts. Many of the miseries that have beset Americans in recent years have been too complex to easily explain. The near collapse of our economic system, caused by so few but afflicting so many, and the confusion and distortion surrounding the raucous, bitter health-care debate have been exploited by talk show hosts and partisan politics to fan a rabid ignorance that looks for simpler things to blame.

On the weekend of Avlon's pre-wedding bachelor party in Las Vegas in October 2009, he took some time out to attend a meeting at the Texas Station Hotel and Casino of the Oath Keepers, a group of gun-toting law enforcement officers, military men and hangers-on who had gathered in the desert to reaffirm their oath to defend the Constitution against all enemies—a category some of them apparently believe include President Barack Obama. Avlon assured me, "These people are not stupid. They actually think they are fighting for freedom. They have wrapped up their extremism in George Washington. In a sense that's the hopeful part. The bad part is that people like this are being used in the larger hyper-partisan devilment. As long as they're willing to rile the opposition, some political leaders think that's just fine. But they're creating conditions that can get out of control. There's no understanding that the entire country has an investment in Barack Obama's future."

Reading Avlon's analysis, I was reminded of my time living in Britain when the extremes of nationalism and religion took Northern Ireland into thirty years of violence from which it is only now recovering. And, of course, it was the Irish poet William Butler Yeats who so memorably captured the eternal predicament of oppositional politics:

The best lack all conviction, while the worst
Are full of passionate intensity.

Yeats's words convey the menace that can explode into bloodshed and violence when that intensity gathers unchecked force. And Avlon does see something menacing in today's Wingnut phenomenon.

Yes, we've had rabid radio shouters and dangerous demagogues before. We had Father Coughlin and the Kingfish, Huey Long, railing against Franklin Roosevelt. We had Joe McCarthy's incitements in the time of Dwight D. Eisenhower, who would become a great president but yet, in the clamor of the 1952 campaign, on one sad day felt unable to defend the honor of one of his benefactors, General George Marshall, an American patriot and a brilliant secretary of state, whom McCarthy had foully denounced as "steeped in falsehood."

What is new is the multiplying reach and volume of the Internet, concentrating the toxicity of destructive emotions and circulating them in the political bloodstream with unparalleled velocity. That, and the fact that our contemporary Father Coughlins are now in control of the megaphone of 24/7 cable and radio talk shows. In a conversation with Avlon about his manuscript, he pointed out that political extremism is not the way America was built. "Most of the great Americans who have led our country to better times in peace and in war have not been polarizers, pitting left against right. They have been centrists who had moved the country forward, not sideways or backwards—in the White House, Theodore Roosevelt, Harry Truman, Dwight

Eisenhower, John Kennedy, but also in the Senate, with centrist figures like Daniel Patrick Moynihan of New York and Margaret Chase Smith of Maine, the first popularly elected female senator, a Republican who stood up against Joe McCarthy."

Avlon is an Independent who describes himself as "fiscally conservative but socially progressive." But he believes that the old labels don't fit anymore, that they fail to illuminate our unprecedented polarization—not just in politics but in the media, too. "We are self-segregating in our news habits, going to either Fox or MSNBC, with CNN, which I admire, sticking to a middle course that is too neutral for our times. I've written *Wingnuts,* against both left and right extremes, because I believe we should see the extremes for what they are and attack them—the Wingnuts of the left as much as the Wingnuts of the right. Nobody can even agree on a common reality anymore, and it leaves the rest of the American public totally confused. My conviction from observing the disintegration of our politics for some years now is that an attempt at a bland bipartisanship is just not enough."

CBS's Ed Murrow may have been over-celebrated as the principled observer for the masses, fair yet unafraid to take on the bullies. But Avlon's beef is that no one even aspires to be Ed Murrow anymore. "The media we have today is a crucial element in the polarization. It's not at all interested in discerning the good and bad points of a policy so much as drumming up dissent and feeding an extremist audience with the raw meat it needs to sustain its paranoia. Because audiences have been built that way, because that's where the profits lie, they have a vested interest creating niche audiences of the like-minded. It may be entertaining, but it is certainly not enlightening."

Fortunately, John Avlon's *Wingnuts* is both.

A WINGNUT GLOSSARY

9/11 Truthers: Conspiracy theorists from both the far right and far left who believe that the terrorist attacks of September 11, 2001, were an inside job.

Birthers: The term used to describe people who believe Barack Obama was born in Kenya and therefore is not constitutionally eligible to serve as president of the United States.

Bush Derangement Syndrome: Defined by columnist Charles Krauthammer as "the acute onset of paranoia in otherwise normal people in reaction to the policies, the presidency—nay—the very existence of George W. Bush."

Code Pink: A left-wing women's group formed to protest the invasion of Iraq. Code Pink specializes in performance art protests against the federal government and military recruiting stations, with a fondness for screaming during congressional hearings.

Fright Wing: The paranoid politics of fear-mongering and conspiracy theories that occurs on the outer limits, where the far right and the far left start to resemble each other.

Hatriots: Obama-era resurgence of the militia movements of the 1990s, motivated by anti-government conspiracies and Revolutionary War imagery. These self-styled patriots fear the government and hate the president.

John Birch Society: Anti-communist, paleo-conservative group founded in 1958. The group's founder famously labeled President Dwight David Eisenhower a "dedicated, conscious agent of the Communist conspiracy." Despite drawing the rebuke of William F. Buckley, Jr., founder of the *National Review,* and other prominent conservatives, the group persists in "End the Fed" and "U.S. out of U.N." efforts.

Know-Nothings: A Nativist political movement in the 1850s that opposed Irish Catholic immigration, it subsequently morphed into the short-lived American Party. Some later anti-immigrant movements have been dubbed the "new Know-Nothings."

League of the South: Founded in 1994, the League of the South advocates for the "independence of the Southern people" from the "American empire."

Lyndon LaRouche: A conspiracy theorist, quasi-cult leader and several-time presidential candidate, whose followers pushed Obama-as-Hitler posters and pamphlets during 2009's health-care debate.

Oath Keepers: An alliance of current and former military personnel and law enforcement officers who pledge to abide by their oath to defend the Constitution. The group stands armed and ready should another American revolution arise.

Obama Derangement Syndrome: Pathological hatred of President Obama, posing as patriotism.

RINO: Republican in Name Only, a label applied by absolutist conservative activists against any Republican who does not fit their fiscal and social conservative litmus test.

Rules for Radicals: A book by Chicago community organizer Saul Alinsky, which laid out a strategy for creating the conditions to achieve revolutionary social change. Its confrontational tactics have recently been adopted by conservative protesters.

Tenthers: 10th Amendment advocates who believe that the federal government has exceeded its constitutional jurisdiction and that therefore states have a right to secede from the Union. Supporters have recently passed "sovereignty" resolutions in eight states.

Three Percenters: A militia-inspired group that takes its name from the questionable statistic that only 3 percent of the American colonists actively fought for independence. It embraces the philosophy of the American Resistance Movement—a survivalist network that teaches its followers how to train for the fight against U.S. Government–led tyranny.

WorldNetDaily: A right-wing Web site founded in 1997 that mixes reporting and opinion and reaches eight million people a month. It is often cited by conspiracy theorists as a prime news source.

I didn't vote for him, but he's my president, and I hope he does a good job.

—John Wayne after the election of John F. Kennedy, 1960

I hope he fails.

—Rush Limbaugh after the election of Barack Obama, 2008

INTRODUCING THE WINGNUTS

A bad craziness snaked through America in the first year of the Obama administration.

"Obama is raping America. Obama is raping our values. Obama is raping our democracy."[1] That's the judgment of Michael Savage, and it's the kind of talk that draws in 9 million listeners, making him one of the top conservative radio hosts in the country.

On the left, MSNBC's Ed Schultz declares: "The Republicans lie. They want to see you dead. They'd rather make money off your dead corpse. They kind of like it when that woman has cancer and they don't have anything for us."[2]

Billy Glassberg believes President Obama is "a traitor and a tyrant." He doesn't have a talk show, but he is affiliated with the Oath Keepers, a group of armed law enforcement officers, military men, and hangers-on who meet to reaffirm their oath to defend the Constitution against all enemies, foreign and domestic—a category that some of them believe includes President Barack Obama.

"The whole point of the Oath Keepers is to stop a dictatorship from ever happening here," says its founder,

Stewart Rhodes, a Yale Law School graduate, former army paratrooper, and former aide to Congressman Ron Paul. "My focus is on the guys with the guns, because they can't do it without them. . . . We say if the American people decide it's time for a revolution, we'll fight with you."[3]

Welcome to life on the freak beat. For the past year, I've been reporting on the outbreak of hyper-partisanship in what was supposed to be the post-partisan Obama era. From the spring's Revolutionary War–inspired Tea Party protests to the summer's health-care town hall hijackings, reasoned policy opposition is being overshadowed by apocalyptic accusations. The president is called both Hitler and a communist. Hope has turned into hate. The Wingnuts are on the attack.

What's a Wingnut? It's someone on the far-right wing or far-left wing of the political spectrum. They are the professional partisans and the unhinged activists, the hard-core haters and the paranoid conspiracy theorists. And they are on the rise.

Pumped up by the self-segregated echo chamber of talk radio, cable news and the Internet, Wingnuts see politics as ideological bloodsport, an all-or-nothing struggle for the nation's soul. They find purpose by dividing America into "us against them." And for those with a vested interest in stirring the crazy-pot, all this is good for business. Hate is a cheap and easy recruiting tool. But it can be murder on a democracy.

The Wingnuts are taking flight amid the anxieties of

leader appealing to popular desires

an economy in manic recession, double-digit unemployment, deep deficits and a decade of war. Demagogues always rise when the economy goes south, offering a narcotic for the nervous and dispossessed, with occasionally violent side effects. During the Great Depression, populist anger was directed at big business. When conservative populism reared its head in the late 1960s, anger shifted toward big government. But now we've got both—anger at big business and big government. It's a perfect political storm, primed for a return to pitchfork politics.

I am not a Democrat. I am not a Republican. I'm an American. I believe the far left and far right are equally insane. But in the opening years of the Obama administration, the Wingnuts on the right have been screaming the loudest.

In some ways, this was predictable. Parties out of power are often dominated by their most extreme voices. Without the responsibility of governing to ground them, ideological activists preach absolutism. They try to demonize and delegitimize the new president from day one—there is no constructive assumption of goodwill, only a permanent opposition campaign. We saw this destructive dynamic at work during George W. Bush's administration, when far-left protests erupted into Bush Derangement Syndrome, comparing Bush to Hitler and calling for impeachment. Now the far right is out of power and, for some of them, losing an election feels like living under tyranny.

loudest = 3rd + weakest

right = conservative (R)
left = liberal (D)

Obama Derangement Syndrome is proliferating—
pathological hatred of the president posing as patriotism.
The people afflicted believe there is a sinister socialist
plot to undermine our Constitutional Republic. It's a
hyper-partisan message hammered home on our airwaves and the Internet with apocalyptic urgency.

The presence of the first African-American president
is driving another anxiety—the change from a tradi-
tionally white to minority-led federal government. Race
has been a core wound in American politics since the
original sin of slavery, but I don't believe that simple
racism is motivating most opposition to Obama. Instead,
there is a fear that our national heritage might be
eclipsed by the rise of a non-white majority in America
by mid-century. We are witnessing the birth of white
minority politics.

As I've traveled across the country interviewing the
luminaries and low-lights among the Wingnuts, I've
heard a consistent refrain: Armageddon days are here
again.

On a Saturday morning in October 2009, I joined the
Oath Keepers for their first annual meeting at the Texas
Station Hotel and Casino, on the fringe of the Las Vegas
strip. In a ballroom beside slot machines and frontier
town façades, nearly 100 current and former military
and law enforcement officers met to reaffirm their constitutional oath.

On the side tables, there were images of a black-
masked storm trooper standing behind the presidential

podium with a skull imposed on the U.S. Capitol dome. There was talk of an H1N1 vaccine conspiracy, false flag operations and concentration camps—all part of a carefully planned descent into fascism and then communism.

Former Arizona sheriff Richard Mack—a militia hero in the 1990s and advisor to the Oath Keepers—feels the anger is justified. "The very people who promised us that they would protect our Constitution are the ones destroying it." He believes President Obama violates his constitutional oath "on a daily basis . . . probably two or three times a day."

Billy Glassberg, a Nevada deli owner, counts Sheriff Mack among his heroes. He's sporting a bright yellow "Don't Tread on Me" T-shirt with a snakeskin cap pulled across his head and headphones around his neck, and tells me earnestly: "There is a fascist takeover of America happening right now. They're trying to destroy the Constitution, enslave the American people and create a one-world government."

Garrett Lear, the so-called Patriot Pastor, nods his head. Dressed in navy blue eighteenth-century regalia, complete with a tricornered hat, the frequent speaker at Tea Party protests believes that "Mr. Obama" is a "domestic enemy" as set forth by the U.S. Constitution and should be impeached. "I have a hard time calling him president though I do want to pay him respect as a human being," intones the six-foot-seven-inch Mayflower descendant, "but I don't personally believe that he's legitimately president of the United States."

The Oath Keepers' first meeting had been held just six months before at Lexington, Massachusetts, on the date and site of the start of the American Revolution, on what is also the anniversary of the Oklahoma City bombing. Now there are more than 3,000 dues-paying members. They are far from the only folks singing from this hymnal. There are other Hatriot groups like the Three Percenters—who take their name from the questionable statistic that only 3 percent of the American population during the Revolutionary War participated as combatants—who are dedicated to staying armed and ready for the next civil war while Tenth Amendment activists, known as Tenthers, make constitutional cases for taking another stab at secession.

This is not just a fringe festival. There are prominent voices fanning the flames. Former Republican House majority leader Dick Armey has taken a lead role organizing the Tea Party protests, and he rallies crowds by first reaffirming their worst fears: "Nearly every important office in Washington, D.C., today is occupied by someone with an aggressive dislike for our heritage, our freedom, our history and our Constitution."[4]

Popular broadcasters amp up the outrage to increase their ratings. Fox News host Glenn Beck announces that America is on the road to socialism, fascism and communism—take your pick—with the kicker: "The country *may not survive* Barack Obama."[5] Conservative talk radio show host Mark Levin, whose book *Liberty and Tyranny* topped the best-seller list, ups the ante by

war with American people

telling his audience, "Obama is literally at war with the American people."[6] Protest signs echo Rush Limbaugh's on-air riffs: "If al-Qaeda wants to demolish the America we know and love, they better hurry, because Obama's beating them to it."[7]

All this anger can have an impact. At Camp Lejeune, North Carolina, twenty-year-old Marine Lance Corporal Kody Brittingham wrote a letter explaining his intention to assassinate Barack Obama: "My vow was to protect against all enemies, both foreign and domestic. I have found, through much research, evidence to support my current state of mind. Having found said domestic enemy, it is my duty and honor to carry out by all means necessary to protect my nation and her people from this threat."[8] He called his plan Operation Patriot.

By pumping up hate in the service of hyper-partisanship, our country is playing with forces that can easily get out of control. We are giving cover—and sometimes a sense of purpose—to the crazy among us. We are encouraging a culture of extremism.

extremism

American political history has been marked periodically by eruptions of "heated exaggeration, suspiciousness and conspiratorial fantasy" that Richard Hofstadter famously characterized as "the paranoid style in American politics."

The Know-Nothing Party of the 1850s was anti-immigrant and anti-Catholic while waving the American flag. President Teddy Roosevelt coined the term "lunatic fringe" to describe the Wingnuts of his day, like the left-wing anarchist who assassinated his predecessor, William McKinley. In the 1920s, the Ku Klux Klan had nearly four million members dedicated to hating not just African-Americans and the prospect of racial "mongrelization" but also Catholics and Jews and the modern Sodoms and Gomorrahs of American cities that violated the Sabbath. During the Great Depression, divisive demagogues like Huey Long on the left and Father Charles Coughlin on the right were hugely popular. Wingnuts surfaced in the militant anti-communism of Joe McCarthy and the John Birch Society. They were flapping their wings when far-left liberals got misty-eyed talking about "Uncle Joe" Stalin. In the '60s, there were pro-segregation White Citizens Councils in the South and more than 1,000 shootings, arsons and bombings from left-wing radical groups like the Black Panthers.[9]

Past presidents have also been the target of unhinged anger. Lincoln was not the first to be called a tyrant, though he was the first to be assassinated for it. FDR was called a communist and a socialist on the floor of the Congress. Eisenhower was accused of being "a dedicated, conscious agent of the Communist conspiracy" by John Birch Society founder Robert Welch. Before his murder, John F. Kennedy was accused of treason, being soft on communism and surrendering the sovereignty of the United States to the United Nations. Ronald Reagan was compared to Hitler by some on the far left at peace protests.

The old Wingnut themes re-circulate and endure through enthusiastic new dupes. Hofstadter identified their core complaints a half century ago: "America has been largely taken away from them and their kind, though they are determined to try to repossess it and to prevent the final destructive act of subversion. The old American virtues have already been eaten away by cosmopolitans and intellectuals; the old competitive capitalism has been gradually undermined by socialist and communist schemers; the old security and independence have been destroyed by treasonous plots having as their most powerful agents not merely outsiders and foreigners but major statesmen seated at the very center of the American power."[10] These claims are echoed in Wingnut protests against President Obama today: America is in rapid decline from an idealized past, subverted by a secret socialist plot, directed by disloyal elites at the heart of the U.S. government.

not logical

There are plenty of rational reasons to oppose President Obama's policies and a real need to propose alternative solutions, but Wingnut politics is not about solving problems. Armed with ideological certainty, they come to protest and polarize. Wingnuts are addicted to their drug of choice—a righteous indignation that makes them unable to see any perspective other than their own.

Wingnuts are sometimes dismissed as simply crazy or eccentric color on the fringes of the political landscape.

*Crazy
Sometimes*

Some partisan leaders play to their fears but consider them useful idiots who can be deployed to attack opponents while maintaining plausible deniability. In the past, Wingnuts' anger and absurdity have been barriers to mainstream acceptance, but their influence is growing.

As our political parties have become more polarized, the Wingnuts have gotten more powerful. The Internet has made it easier for Wingnuts to communicate and congregate, forming online armies. At the same time, the rigged system of partisan redistricting has pushed power from the center to the margins of our politics. This combination has amplified the voices of the extremes and given them disproportionate influence, making them, in effect, the loudest lobbying bloc and creating real leverage on party leadership.

The fringe is now blurring with the base, enforcing a bitter and predictable partisanship. The most influential figures are political entertainers like Rush Limbaugh and Glenn Beck—they are leaders without the responsibility of governing, a combination that encourages the demonization of difference and the condemnation of compromise. Now elected officials are starting to follow their model, mimicking talk radio's confrontational style in an attempt to achieve Wingnut folk-hero status.

So Republican Congressman Trent Franks calls President Obama "an enemy of humanity."[11] And Democratic Congressman Alan Grayson calls Republicans "the enemy of America."[12] No matter how indefensible their comments, they are reflexively defended by partisans on their side of the aisle—"My party, right or wrong" is replacing "My country, right or wrong."

It wasn't supposed to be this way. Think back to 2008.

Barack Obama campaigned as the antidote to the polarized politics of the past, promising to transcend the old divides of left and right, black and white, red states and blue states. *Wanted to break barriers*

He introduced himself to the American people in 2004 by saying, "There's not a liberal America and a conservative America; there's the United States of America."

His first ad for president began by professing "We are one people" (an implicit dis to John Edwards' "two Americas" riff) and then went on to establish his bipartisan bona fides, claiming that "In Illinois, he brought Republicans and Democrats together, cutting taxes for workers and winning health care for children," followed by a testimonial from a Republican state senator.[13]

In his stump speech during the run-up to his Iowa caucus victory, Obama hammered home the same themes: "We have the chance to build a new majority of not just Democrats, but Independents and Republicans. . . . We can change the electoral math that's been all about division and make it about addition."[14]

While his rhetoric tacked toward the center, his voting record veered left. In this, Obama became something of a Rorschach test—people could project whatever politics they wanted onto him. But even his Gen X biography reinforced the centrist message: His baby boomer mother married a Kenyan; his grandparents voted for Nixon—Barack tried to bridge the divide. To his supporters, Barack Obama embodied an ability to unite the nation.

On the right, John McCain's nomination was a repudiation of the world according to Karl Rove. Instead of pursuing a play-to-the-base strategy, courting evangelicals and conservative activists, the maverick Arizona senator stressed his record of independence from the Bush administration, his consistent commitment to fiscal responsibility and his appeal to independent voters. With the incumbent Republican president polling at 25 percent and 81 percent of Americans believing the nation was moving in the wrong direction, McCain was facing an uphill fight. But that was nothing new: The man was a walking profile in courage—a top-gun fighter pilot shot down over Vietnam and a defiant survivor of five years in a POW camp. McCain's political profile was forged in opposition to the Bush 2000 campaign, as much as it was in the Hanoi Hilton. The religious right had never forgiven him for this statement during that bitter primary fight: "Neither party should be defined by pandering to the outer reaches of American politics and the agents of intolerance whether they be Louis Farrakhan or Al Sharpton on the left, or Pat Robertson or Jerry Falwell on the right."[15] McCain's independence made him suspect to conservative activists—they considered him a collaborator when he formed bipartisan coalitions in the Senate and disloyal when he dared to criticize conservatives in Congress for pork barrel spending. Despite the long odds against winning the Republican nomination, the old gambler proved that there was still strength in the center of the GOP.

But even with nominees who campaigned on reaching out across partisan divides, the ugly outliers of politics found a way to weasel back in. Candidate Obama was prescient when he predicted that "they're going to try and make me into a scary guy."[16] The seeds of hate were sown during the late innings of the election, with Sarah Palin's "palling around with terrorists," "socialist" and "real America" rants. The specter of race bubbled up ugly from the grassroots while anonymous e-mail campaigns trafficked in Muslim rumors. Of course, unhinged anger was not exclusive to the right. On the Democrats' side, the "God damn America!" tape of Reverend Jeremiah Wright validated many fears. Madonna juxtaposed images of McCain and Palin with Hitler and Idi Amin in her concert tour. Sarah Palin was hanged in effigy as part of a Hollywood Halloween display without much media outcry.

But on Election Day, Obama won virtually every swing state and independents by eight points. He won 90 percent of liberals, 60 percent of centrists and even 20 percent of self-described conservatives.[17] Obama's 53 percent of the popular vote was more than any president

BIG Win
large %.

in twenty years and more than any twentieth-century Democrat except Franklin Delano Roosevelt and Lyndon Johnson.[18] It seemed to be a clear mandate for change away from the harshly polarized politics of the past.

There was just one problem—the hard-core partisans were not about to abandon their positions without a fight. They *like* play-to-the-base politics. They profit from it personally and professionally. And they were going to perpetuate the "us against them" era by any means necessary.

Neither side was in the mood for compromise. They had partisan networks and netroots dedicated to their cause that could be deployed almost at will. With liberal Republicans extinct and conservative Democrats an increasingly endangered species, there was no internal big tent counterbalance. Like-minded groups are always more likely to move to the extremes. The new president's post-partisan vision was dismissed as naïve, if necessary, campaign rhetoric. A few weeks in Washington would teach him how things were done—post-partisanship would be DOA in D.C.

And so a guerrilla war broke out in American politics, organized on the Internet and fought out on the airwaves and in town halls, cultivating the wounds of the 2008 campaign and pouring gasoline on the embers of the culture wars. To some in the conservative resistance, President Obama is anti-American, pushing us toward National Socialism; to others—the so-called Birthers—he is un-American, literally ineligible for office according to the Constitution. A July 2009 poll found that 58 percent of Republicans either thought Barack Obama wasn't born in the United States or weren't sure.[19]

We saw this destructive dynamic at work during the previous administration, when far-left protests erupted into Bush Derangement Syndrome. Obama haters always eventually say the same thing: "They started it." The prevalence of Bush Derangement Syndrome on the left gave the right the green light to escalate. Coinage credit goes to conservative columnist and trained psychiatrist Charles Krauthammer, who in 2003 had diagnosed the condition as "the acute onset of paranoia in otherwise normal people in reaction to the policies, the presidency—nay—the very existence of George W. Bush."[20]

It began with the left's belief that Bush was an illegitimate president, rooted in the bitterly contested results of the 2000 election. He'd lost the popular vote and won with an assist from the Supreme Court. Fresh from the Florida recount—where 97,000 leftist protest votes for Ralph Nader helped deliver the Sunshine State to George W. Bush by a 537-vote margin[21]—Inauguration Day protesters wielded "Hail to the Thief" signs and chanted "Racist, sexist, anti-gay, Bush and Cheney go away!" "We want Bush out of D.C." and "You're not our president."

Bush Derangement Syndrome, though, was slower to boil than Obama Derangement Syndrome. In the wake of 9/11, the far left's insatiable appetite for moral equivalency made little impact, but, of course, the blame-

America-first crowd did their best. Two weeks after the attacks, nearly 10,000 assembled for a protest in Washington, inevitably titled the Anti-War and Anti-Racist Rally, to imbibe Wingnut wisdom from such as the Reverend Graylan Hagler, senior minister of the Plymouth Congregational United Church of Christ in Washington, D.C. ("Today we do not stand with any terrorists, whether it is the United States or foreign terrorists"[22]), or Stephanie Simard from the Women's Fight Back Union ("Millions of women and children around the world wake up to this kind of terror every single day. And this terror is made in the United States. . . . Bush's program is anti-women, anti-gay, and anti a lot of us.") I wonder how she would have liked the Taliban by comparison.

The Iraq war proved a potent recruitment tool. Michael Moore's 2004 film *Fahrenheit 9/11* mixed provocative footage of Bush's missteps and malapropisms along with a full range of conspiracy theories concerning the Bush family's ties to the Saudi royal family and the bin Laden family, documenting a case of blood for oil. It won the Palme d'Or at the Cannes Film Festival. In 2006, the movie *Death of a President,* a mockumentary of sorts, purported to follow the investigation of the unsolved assassination of George W. Bush and the subsequent expansion of the Patriot Act by President Dick Cheney. It won the International Critics Prize at the Toronto Film Festival.

The left-Wingnut netroots paraded their Bush hate, such as this post at the leading left-wing political Web site Daily Kos: "I know hate is a strong word. But I do hate the man. I hate him."[23] Groups like Code Pink staged "die-ins," screamed during congressional hearings, protested military recruitment stations and attempted citizen's arrests of administration officials. A collection of memorable signs from the anti-Bush protests gives you a sense of the derangement: "Bush = Satan," "Save Mother Earth, Kill Bush," "Hang Bush for War Crimes," "End the Illegal Occupation in the White House," "Bush is the Disease, Death is the Cure," "Bush is the only Dope worth Shooting," "Death to Extremist Christian Terrorist Pig Bush," and "Kill Terrorists, Bomb There [sic] House, Kill Bush, Bomb His F——-in House." The "s" in Bush's name was routinely turned into a swastika on protest posters and the tell-tale tiny mustache drawn upon his image.

But Bush-as-Hitler comparisons did not just gain currency on protest placards—this was Café Society stuff. The 2005 winner of the Nobel Prize for Literature, British playwright Harold Pinter, penned a statement saying, "The Bush administration is the most dangerous force that has ever existed. It is more dangerous than Nazi Germany because of the range and depth of its activities and intentions worldwide."[24] Liberal author and one-time Al Gore clothing consultant Naomi Wolf offered comparisons of the Bush administration to the Nazi regime in her book *The End of America* (an assertion benignly recounted in an interview on NPR titled "Naomi Wolf Likens Bush to Hitler"[25]). MSNBC *Countdown* host Keith

Olbermann called Bush a fascist on air,[26] while Moveon.org took heat for an online advertising contest where two contributors offered Bush = Hitler comparisons.

Legendary singer, civil rights leader and Hollywood elder statesman Harry Belafonte traveled to visit Venezuelan dictator Hugo Chávez and announced: "No matter what the greatest tyrant in the world, the greatest terrorist in the world, George W. Bush says, we're here to tell you: Not hundreds, not thousands, but millions of the American people . . . support your revolution."[27] Antiwar protester and mother of fallen soldier Cindy Sheehan became a brief media sensation for camping out near Bush's Crawford ranch—a status not considerably diminished when she followed Belafonte's lead by calling President Bush "a bigger terrorist than Osama bin Laden."[28]

When Nobel Peace Prize winner Betty Williams of Northern Ireland gave the keynote speech to the International Women's Peace Conference in Dallas, she said, "Right now, I could kill George Bush, no problem. No, I don't mean that. I mean—how could you nonviolently kill somebody? I would love to be able to do that."[29] She chuckled a bit in her confessional Irish brogue, and members of the audience laughed. Not that Dallas has any history with presidential assassinations.

Democrats didn't seem allergic to these outbursts, they seemed instead subtly to encourage them for partisan gain—just as they accuse Republicans of doing now.

Bush Derangement Syndrome was so widespread on the left—and Bush so broadly unpopular by the end of his term—that it failed to inspire much mainstream media outrage. It wasn't considered news. *not even news*

But after one Bush-bashing protest in September 2005, Fox News host Sean Hannity had an admirable if unusual moment of clarity: "The president was called every name in the book—from a terrorist to the Führer," he said, shaking his head, and then turned his attention to one of the protest's liberal organizers. "If you really believe what you're saying, you need to distance yourself from the extremists that are running this thing."[30]

It was good advice—then and now. *distance from extremists*

We are caught in a pendulum swing of hyper-partisanship. The extremes echo and incite each other, confirming their side's worst stereotypes while providing the most potent recruitment poster for the other party. Politics follows the lines of physics—every action creates an equal and opposite reaction.

Wingnuts on the right are intimidating responsible Republicans into silence. The hunt for heretics has become a hobby for right-wing activists in an effort to drive all centrists out of the GOP. They are burning down the big tent. The roots of this new radicalism can be found in the anger of an increasingly regional party facing a deep diversity deficit, reflecting an historic irony: Republicans are now captive to the southern conservatives their party was founded to oppose. The Party of Lincoln is in danger of becoming the Party of Limbaugh.

But Democrats have their own extremes to contend with, and they're in control of Congress, provoking a backlash by pursuing a more liberal and narrowly partisan agenda than President Obama promised in the campaign. Invigorated by the unprecedented growth of government spending, the liberal House leadership and their netroot allies are pressuring the president to abandon any outreach to Republicans—despite the fact it was this hyper-partisan approach to politics that caused independents to abandon President Bush.

As the two parties become more polarized, the ranks of independent voters have rocketed to a historic high since Inauguration Day—reaching more than 40 percent[31]—while Democrats and Republicans have declined dramatically. Independents are now the largest and fastest-growing segment of the electorate.

Independents are fiscal conservatives but social progressives. They more accurately reflect centrist national attitudes than either party's base: the 11 percent of Americans who describe themselves as liberal Democrats or the 15 percent who call themselves conservative Republicans.[32] Independents care more about the country than the success of any one political party. Their growth amid a bailout backlash is evidence that President Obama's election did not represent a liberal ideological mandate, as House Democrats and their partisan cheerleaders might wish—there is no blank check for spending or the unlimited growth of government.

But it also shows that rejection of the Republican brand has accelerated since Rush Limbaugh and Sarah Palin became the most prominent public faces of their party. It is a sign of Americans' persistent demand for non-ideological problem solving even in this us-against-them era. We are not as divided as we think we are. (and minority)

Our politics are being hijacked by a comparatively small number of people who seek to dominate the debate by screaming the loudest. They see the world as an urgent struggle between true believers and nonbelievers. They attempt to impose strict litmus tests and insist on conformity. They demonize dissent and consider all political opponents their enemies. Fear is their favorite tactic as they try to divide and conquer.

At a time when America is fighting a war against extremism abroad, we are confronting extremism at home. We should know the dangers of demagogues, politicized religion and ideological absolutists by now. The cultivation of rage and resentment for political gain or personal profit has real costs that can affect us all.

The attack of the Wingnuts is an assault on the idea that what unites us is greater than what divides us as Americans, which the Founding Fathers enshrined in our national motto, *e pluribus unum*—out of many, one. The moderate majority needs to stand up to the extremes before they spark a season of violence. We have done this before and we can do it again, remembering what the old warrior President Eisenhower once said: "The middle of the road is all the usable surface. The extremes, left and right, are in the gutters."[33]

OF TEA PARTIES AND TOWN HALLS

It started with the rant heard round the world.

CNBC's Rick Santelli was railing against President Obama's mortgage bailout plan from the floor of the Chicago Mercantile Exchange. It was February 19, 2009—one day short of the president's first month in office. And Santelli was pissed.

"This is America!" Santelli screamed. "How many of you people want to pay for your neighbor's mortgage that has an extra bathroom and can't pay their bills? Raise your hand." The question was met with a motley chorus of boos from the traders, kicking Santelli into high-gear capitalist evangelist mode: "President Obama," Santelli shouted straight into the camera, "Are you listening?"[1] There was a roar of recognition from the floor.

"This is like mob rule, I'm getting scared," blow-dried co-host Joe Kernen joked nervously. He hadn't seen nothin' yet.

"We're thinking of having a Chicago Tea Party in July," yelled Santelli. "All you capitalists that want to show up to Lake Michigan, I'm going to start organizing."

Within twelve hours ChicagoTeaParty.com was live.

There had been Tea Party protests as part of libertarian Republican Ron Paul's 2008 presidential campaign. And a protest over "Porkulus" (a Rush Limbaugh-coined word combining "pork" and "stimulus") had been held a few days before in Seattle at the suggestion of a blogger who went by the name Liberty Belle. But the call for a Tea Party on live television, with all its American Revolution imagery was immediately resonant.

On February 27, some 300 people gathered in Chicago's Daley Plaza to protest the stimulus bill and government spending, with gatherings in forty other cities. People in parkas stood alongside protesters dressed in Revolutionary-era outfits wielding "Don't Tread on Me" flags. There was also the first post-election protest sighting of an Obama poster with a Hitler mustache pasted on. The word "change" now read "chaos."[2] A spark had been lit. right away

Congressional Democrats fanned the flames, voting to spend an unprecedented 1.2 trillion in taxpayer dollars in the first 100 days of the Obama administration. Their plans promised to double the public debt in five years, equivalent to all the debt accumulated by every U.S. president from George Washington to George W. Bush combined.[3]

It seemed to validate every slumbering "socialist" accusation leveled at Obama during the campaign, but liberal House Democrats didn't care—they hadn't enjoyed unified control for fifteen years. This was their chance to run the table with a long-delayed wish list of pork barrel projects. They thought the economic crisis and Bush's backing of the first bailout round gave them perfect political cover. Keynesianism was suddenly cool again, and with it they could justify a smorgasbord of spending. It would all pay for itself, after all.

They had forgotten that hypocrisy is the unforgivable sin in politics. Obama had campaigned on a commitment to be a post-partisan president and restore fiscal responsibility. But the $787 billion stimulus bill passed along narrow partisan lines, with Republicans shut out of the negotiating process. Despite the president's hopes of gaining Republican support, the House bill received no GOP votes and lost the support of eleven centrist Democrats.[4] Weeks later, when an additional $410 billion supplemental spending bill was passed along partisan lines with 9,000 earmarks,[5] Obama's campaign promise of transparency seemed to have been abandoned as well.

Bailout backlash was in full effect. It didn't matter that the giveaway had started under Bush—the man left holding the bag got the blame. The economy had been in free fall for four months when Obama was inaugurated. Then it got worse, with the stock market hitting a twelve-year low on his fiftieth day in office, March 9th. With unemployment rising, 401(k)s decimated, but billions of taxpayer dollars going to banks and Wall Street bonuses, Americans began to have a collective Howard Beale moment—they were mad as hell and not going to take it anymore.

The deep deficit spending seemed only to add insult
to injury. After watching the jet-set excesses of the
Bernie Madoff class from afar, middle-class families were
left with less and still asked to clean up the mess. While
they were struggling to pay their bills, big government
and big business had their debts forgiven through billion-dollar backroom deals on the taxpayers' backs. Big
mistake. In 1992, independents protested the bipartisan
deficit spending they considered generational theft by
backing the independent presidential candidacy of Ross
Perot. By March of '09, independents began to break de-
cisively with Obama, surpassing Democrats as the
largest segment of the electorate. They were sending a
clear message: It's the Spending, Stupid.

On Tax Day, April 15, Tea Party protests were held in
346 towns and cities, drawing more than 300,000 people.[6] The largest gathering was in Atlanta, where 15,000
showed up. Liberal columnists and MSNBC hosts joined
with Speaker of the House Nancy Pelosi in trying to
downplay the events, dismissing them as artificial "Astroturf" protests rather than a genuine grassroots movement. True, groups like Americans for Prosperity and
FreedomWorks helped fund organizational costs,[7] while
Fox News helped make the protests a national conservative happening by airing more than 100 commercial pro-
motions for the protests in the ten days before Tax Day,[8]
but these were the equivalent of conservative public
service announcements. For all the "Astroturf" asides,
the crowds were home-grown. They may have been

Tea Parties

pumped up by partisan interests, but they were not purchased.

I went to the New York City Tea Party, where given the city's Democratic dominance I expected to see a few hundred people clustered under a gray sky. Instead, 3,500 people, a kaleidoscope of the modern conservative movement, lined both sides of Broadway beside City Hall Park, a few blocks from Wall Street. There were libertarians, traditionalists, free-marketers, middle-class tax protesters, the more-patriotic-than-thou crowd, conservative shock jocks, frat boys, suit-and-tie Buckley-ites and more than a couple of requisite residents of Crazytown.

The Tax Day Tea Parties offered a perfect confluence for conservative populism: a Founding Fathers–sanctioned rebellion against big government combined with the age-old frustration of paying taxes, especially during a recession. And compared with the average G-20 or WTO protests, the New York rally was a model of civil disobedience. Instead of anarcho-punks leaving broken windows in their wake, there were American flags, country music and repeated reminders to pick up trash before leaving the site. There were whole families on parade, such as the father carrying the American flag with an image of John Wayne emblazoned on it, followed by three children with pint-size "Don't Tread on Me" flags (a sentiment that also doubled as a crowd-control notice).

The founder of the New York Tea Party Patriots chapter was a soft-spoken twenty-seven-year-old aspiring architect named Kellen Giuda. A New Hampshire native, he'd never been active in politics before, but the spending spurred him into action, coordinating the initial rally over Facebook. Kellen define the overall Tea Party message as "fiscal responsibility and government accountability," adding, "In New York, we're strictly fiscal responsibility but if the Morristown, New Jersey, Tea Party wants to be anti-abortion then that's their prerogative." He stressed that "there is no Tea Party leader" and that both parties have failed when it comes to fighting for the taxpayer. "That's why a lot of Tea Parties around the country have considered starting a political party."

But while speaker after speaker hammered home the apparently poll-tested line that these rallies were not about Republicans or Democrats, their appeal was self-evidently partisan to the extent that it was strenuously anti-Obama.

"What's the Difference Between Obama and Chavez?" asked one sign, referring to Hugo Chávez, the president of Venezuela (Answer: "Nothing"). Others went after "Ali Obama and the 40 Thieves," "Free Markets not Free-Loaders," and "Hitler was a Socialist Too." Some messages stood out, such as the Ron Paul acolyte whose sign read "Obama = Bush lite." When I asked about the underlying logic, he explained, "Obama was elected with the promise of change and then pursued the same failed policies of Bush's fiscal irresponsibility."

When speakers extolled the virtue of "individual responsibility," the crowd roared—the billion-dollar bailouts blocked any memory of the president's call for

all in response to bailouts

a "new era of responsibility" in his inaugural address. Democratic stereotypes about being an over-spending party of the welfare state had reasserted themselves. Old scripts felt fresh again, even when they were straw men. When one local radio host asserted, "We are told that if the few prosper, the many will suffer," he was reflexively riffing off old anticommunist playbooks, not anything said by Obama. And when Christian conservative radio personality Jordan Sekulow decried "cutting funding for our troops," he hadn't bothered to read the budget he was busy attacking.

For all the invocations of American history at the protest, there was a striking lack of perspective. However disenfranchised conservatives felt, we are a world away from "taxation without representation"—the closer truth might be found in one woman's hand-painted sign: "taxation with crappy representation." Rolling back the Bush tax cuts to Clinton-era rates—however unwise in a recession—does not put us inexorably on the road to socialism, let alone communism. It reminded me of a Stephen Colbert line: "I love the truth; it's facts I'm not a fan of."

Conservatives were playing the mirror image of the liberals they mocked after 2000, portraying a popular election as an unconstitutional usurpation of power. But liberals who wanted to dismiss the Tea Parties did so at their peril: Never forget that America was founded in part by a tax revolt.

And this was only the eighty-sixth day of Barack Obama's presidency.

new anger

Right-Wing Rules for Radicals

By summer, politics had gotten even more heated over President Obama's proposed health-care plan—the Holy Grail and third rail of Democratic presidents since Harry Truman.

The Tea Party protesters now focused their energies on the town halls hosted by congressmen every August for their constituents. Normally, these were sleepy affairs, but by the end of the summer they looked more like a collective crystal meth binge than a Norman Rockwell painting.

The roots of the town hall protests were the same as the Tea Parties—anger at the growth of government and the unprecedented spending. The fact that the president had called for the health-care legislation to pass before the August recess felt to many citizens like liberal arrogance and overreach. When liberal Democratic leaders like House Judiciary Committee Chairman John Conyers mocked the idea of actually reading the health-care bill—telling the National Press Club, "What good is reading the bill when it's a thousand pages? And you don't have two days and two lawyers to find out what it means after you've read the bill?"[9]—protesters went ballistic.

"Obama was elected to unify the nation," a plaid-shirted baby boomer named Dan Cochran told me at a town hall in Windsor, Colorado. "And what we've got with health care is the most divisive debate I've seen since Vietnam. They attempted to cram it down our throat overnight with no consideration to We the Taxpayer."

When nervous aides told Dan and the rest of the Colorado crowd that Democratic Congresswoman Betsy Markey would not be appearing at the town hall as advertised (due to a death threat, her press officer quietly told me on the side), the natives went from restless to revolt—they were going to have their hearing with or without the congresswoman. One local farmer rose out of the crowd and offered a laundry list of grievances written out on a pad of paper: "Loss of individual rights; the Deficit; Health Care Cost/Limitation of Choice; Stimulus Plan; Government Bailouts that were not read but passed; Card Check; Fairness Doctrine; CIA investigation; Cap & Trade. Stop the spending. Listen to the people."

These citizens were angry, but they were far from uninformed—they had just gotten their information from partisan sources, professional polarizers like Rush Limbaugh and Glenn Beck, who pump up outrage to pump up ratings. Policy debates now felt like referendums on the future of the republic, with nothing short of tyranny and genocide ahead. But with Democrats in control of Congress and the White House, they felt unheard. And so the screaming started.

Maryland Congressman Frank Kratovil was hanged in effigy outside his office. New York Congressman Tim Bishop had to be escorted to his car by police after one town hall to protect him from the protesters. North Carolina Congressman Brad Miller decided to cancel his August town halls after receiving a death threat. "They're inciting people to riot with just total distortions of facts," said freshman Virginia Representative Gerry Connolly. "They think we're going to euthanize Grandma and the government is going to take over."[10]

The fringe was starting to blur with the base. The curtain was pulled back on this shift in the form of a memo titled "Rocking the Town Halls—Best Practices." Written by a Connecticut grassroots conservative activist named Bob MacGuffie under the banner of his group, Right Principles, the memo tried to teach people how to disrupt the town halls held in support of what was called "the socialist agenda of the Democrat leadership in Washington." In a perfect Wingnut irony, the memo counseled conservatives to "Use the [Saul] Alinsky playbook of which the left is so proud: freeze it, attack it, personalize it and polarize it."

Saul Alinsky was a Chicago community organizer and the author of *Rules for Radicals,* a bible for post-1960s leftist protesters. The book laid out a strategy for creating the conditions to achieve revolutionary social change. As Alinsky explained in the first chapter, "*The Prince* was written by Machiavelli for the Haves on how to hold power. *Rules for Radicals* is written for the Have-Nots on how to take it away." His rules included aphorisms like, "In war the end justifies almost any means," and he advised adherents to obscure their ultimate goals in general, unobjectionable terms like "Liberty, Equality, Fraternity," "Of the Common Welfare" and "Pursuit of Happiness."[11]

Vilified by conservatives and idolized by liberals, Alinsky's impact endured after his death in 1972. Hillary Clinton wrote her ninety-two-page undergraduate thesis at Wellesley on Alinsky, earnestly titled "'There Is Only the Fight . . .': An Analysis of the Alinsky Model." As a young Chicago community organizer, Barack Obama reportedly studied and taught Alinsky's techniques, seeding conservative distrust of his centrist rhetoric. MacGuffie's memo was a minor screed, but it applied the liberal protesters' confrontational approach to conservative goals: "The objective is to put the Rep on the defensive . . . you need to rock the boat early. Watch for an opportunity to yell out and challenge the Rep's statements early. If he blames Bush for something or offers other excuses—call him on it, yell back and have someone else follow up with a shout-out. . . . Look for these opportunities even before he takes questions."

Beyond barraging the congressmen, the goal was to intimidate the undecided:

"We want the independent thinkers to leave the hall with some doubts about the Democrat solutions continually proposed by the national leadership."[12]

This was the decisive shift in conservative opposition tactics in 2009—a decision to mimic the confrontational street theater of the far left they had spent decades despising. Extremes end up resembling each other. Now conservative activists were manning the ramparts, seeing themselves as patriots protesting the president. Civility was the first calculated casualty.

In Connecticut, protesters against Senator Chris Dodd suggested that he commit suicide with whiskey and painkillers as a treatment for his newly diagnosed prostate cancer.[13] One sign summed up their sentiments: "universal health care = medical genocide." Screaming matches became a regular feature of Senator Arlen Specter's town hall meetings in Pennsylvania after he switched parties and became a Democrat in April '09. Choice cuts include: "You are trampling on our Constitution" and "This is the Soviet Union, this is Maoist China. The people in this room want their country back."[14] In Missouri, Senator Claire McCaskill was shouted down repeatedly at a health-care town hall attended by 1,500 people. "I don't understand this rudeness," McCaskill told the crowd. "I honestly don't get it."[15] In Washington State, a retired Marine Corps veteran accused Representative Brian Baird of trying to "indoctrinate" his children and said that Nazis also took over finance and health care: "I've kept my oath. Do you ever intend to keep yours?"

Doctored photos of President Obama as Hitler began popping up at town halls courtesy of longtime political fringe magnet Lyndon LaRouche alongside pamphlets offering details about "Obama's Nazi Health Plan."

Sarah Palin, newly resigned from her position as Alaska's governor, picked up the LaRouche-ite riff and doubled down on the crazy talk with a Facebook post: "The America I know and love is not one in which my parents or my baby with Down syndrome will have to stand in front of Obama's 'death panel' so his bureaucrats can decide, based on a subjective judgment of their 'level of productivity in society,' whether they are worthy of health care. Such a system is downright evil."[16]

Soon the talk of "death panels" and "killing granny" seemed to be everywhere. At a "Patients First" healthcare protest in Pueblo, Colorado, the featured speaker expanded the death-panel argument to genocidal dictators. "Stalin in the 1920s issued about 20 million end of life orders for his fellow Russians. Pol Pot did it in the Vietnam War. He issued about 2 million end of life orders. It's being done in Africa today. Mugabe is doing it every day. Adolf Hitler issued 6 million end of life orders. He called his program the final solution. I kind of wonder what we're going to call ours."[17]

A swastika was spray-painted outside the office of Representative David Scott's office in Georgia. Arizona Representative Gabrielle Giffords's aides called the cops after one town-hall attendee dropped a gun at the event. After Washington Representative Brian Baird was faxed a death threat addressed to President Obama, he declared, "What we're seeing right now is close to Brown Shirt tactics." At a Republican town hall, John McCain received a chorus of angry boos and jeers for simply stating that "Obama respects the Constitution of the United States."[18]

The Tea Party Express was also winding its way through the country. A thirty-four-city tour backed by the conservative political action committee (PAC) Our Country Deserves Better was one of several that sought to carry the banner of the Tea Parties forward, raising $1.9 million in the process.[19] The lead speakers at their rallies were former radio talk show hosts Mark Williams and Deborah Johns. Williams's signature crowd-pleasing line was ripped from the National Rifle Association (NRA): "You can have our country when you pry it from our . . . cold . . . dead . . . fingers!"[20]

Johns aimed a little lower: "The men and women in our military didn't fight and die for this country for a communist in the White House!" The Louisville, Kentucky, crowd chanted their approval: "U-S-A, U-S-A!"[21]

Down in the crowd, two men in fatigues were trying to recruit new members for their militia, the Ohio Valley Freedom Fighters, by carrying signs that read: "AK-47s: today's pitchfork" and "Quit worrying. Start your militia training today."[22]

With all the violent rhetoric, it was perhaps inevitable that actual violence would start breaking out. There were fistfights in Florida town halls alongside senior citizen scuffles.[23] In Missouri, a brawl between Tea Party activists and counter-protesting Service Employees International Union (SEIU) members got one man hospitalized and six arrested.[24] In California, health-care reform opponent Bill Rice had his finger bitten off at a rally sponsored by MoveOn.org. As Rice gamely recounted, "A scuffle ensued and he ate my finger in the process."[25] Things were getting ugly and weird.

The 9/12 March on Washington

After Representative Joe Wilson screamed, "You lie!" at President Obama during his health-care speech in front of a joint session of Congress, Wilson said it was just an extension of the angry outbursts he'd been hearing at town halls back home in South Carolina. It was a feedback loop of anger and alienation.

Wilson was censured by the House for his outburst, becoming the first congressman in 221 years to earn the dishonor, but in return he became an overnight folk hero on the far right. Soon he was raising more than a million dollars by playing the victim card online: "Joe Wilson is Under Attack," the ads read. "Help him fight back." His opponent also raised a million.

Five days after his scream, I saw signs of support dotting the Washington Mall—"Joe Wilson told the Truth," "Joe Wilson speaks for me" and "Palin/Wilson 2012."

The posters were all part of the latest Wingnut Woodstock—the 9/12 march on Washington. The date had been selected by the guru of the growing Tea Party movement, Fox News host Glenn Beck. He pitched it as a day to return to the unity, patriotism and sense of national purpose we felt the day after the attacks of September 11, 2001.

What emerged was something precisely the opposite: a protest that celebrated the deepest domestic political divisions we've seen since 9/11, with unhinged accusations of traitors and despots in the White House and talk of resistance and revolution.

As I walked out of Union Station that morning, I folded into the waves of white people who descended on the Washington Mall. As more than one T-shirt put it, they were exercising their First Amendment rights so they don't have to exercise their Second Amendment rights—yet.

They had the giddy glow of those who feel they are speaking truth to power, a reversal of fortune that had left conservatives recycling some of the Dems' favorite lines from the Bush era: "Obama is a domestic terrorist," "Dissent is patriotic" and the ever proliferating Obama-as-Hitler.

"It's wonderful to see so many patriots here!" shouted one speaker from the podium on the steps of Capitol Hill to a chorus of cheers—and he started to list U.S. battles from Guadalcanal on, won by courageous patriots, not the government, to defend a freedom that he said is now under threat from inside the White House. South Carolina Senator Jim DeMint and Indiana Congressman Mike Pence were among the few elected officials who addressed the crowd.

But the homemade signs on the ground spoke more clearly than many of the speakers. There were appropriations of Obama's red, white and blue "O" symbol inserted into the words "Treason" and "Destroyer." A man dressed as George Washington approvingly nodded at a collage featuring Obama's "best friends"—Karl Marx, Hugo Chávez and Mohammed.

Here is a selection of signs, chosen more or less at random: "Don't Make the U.S. a Third World Country—Go Back to Kenya," "We Came Unarmed (This Time)," "Christians Unite," "Muslim Marxist," "Mugabe-Pelosi in '12," "If you are a liberal or progressive Democrat or Republican you are a communist. Impeach Obama!" "Obama the Exterminator: Killing Our Jobs, Killing Our Future, Killing Our Freedom," "Radical Socialists are Damaged Hate-Filled Power Hungry Destroyers," "Bury ObamaCare with Kennedy," "King George Didn't Listen Either," "God Bless Glenn Beck and Fox News," "Preserve Mom, Apple Pie and the American Way," "Barack Obama Supports Abortion, Sodomy, Socialism and the New World Order," "An Obamanation of Taxation! The Lifeblood of Tyranny!" "Obama Lied, Granny Died," "NObama Healthcare is America's Nightmare" and finally, inevitably, seriously, "Don't Touch My Medicare."

One man sat with his family on the rim of a reflecting pool, brandishing a homemade red Soviet-style flag complete with hammer and sickle, with the words "United States Socialist Republic" on it. He was a Vietnam vet from the Shenandoah Valley who gave his name only as Bob. "I was always afraid of my country being attacked from the outside by bombs and rockets and *being attacked*

missiles," Bob told me. "Now I'm watching it being destroyed from right here. I'm scared for my country." But did he think Obama is a communist? "I think he's a direct threat to my country, but it's not just him. It's the Congress. I think this is all part of a plan. I don't know what he is. I do believe he has socialist tendencies."

Among the crowd were a few scattered Confederate flags flapping in the wind. I went up to one auburn-haired middle-aged woman named Becky and asked why she was carrying the Stars and Bars to the rally. "Because I'm from the South," Becky said. "It has nothing to do with slavery. People think it means slavery. That's not what it stood for. It stood for the Union."

to represent the South

Somewhere, Lincoln just threw up.

A guy named Norm decided to step in and help her out: "I don't think it's so much that anybody would advocate any secession-like movement, or that anybody wants to remove a star from the flag. I think if anything, the Confederate flag serves to remind me of where we've been and where we would not like to go again."

There is a "Don't make me shoot this dog" aspect to this logic: an angry, divisive protest designed to stop the divisions they feel erupting from Washington's policies. It echoed what one young man at the Tea Party Express stop in Jackson, Michigan, told a reporter who asked why he was carrying a loaded AK-47 and two loaded handguns. "I don't want a revolution. I don't want a civil war," he said. "But it is a possibility. It's there as an option, as a last resort."[26]

Liberals who want to ignore the populist anger of the Tea Parties and town halls do so at their political peril—the frustration at Washington overspending is real, a reflection of bailout backlash. People are angry because they are expected to pay their bills and balance their budgets, but both big business and big government seem arrogantly exempt while passing the buck to the next generation.

But Republicans are playing a dangerous game. They are benefiting from all this anger in the short term, but they have tapped into something they can't control. Calling the president a Nazi or communist is something far beyond simple incivility or street theater—it is an accusation that intentionally stirs the crazy pot. It is ultimately an incitement to violence.

- Why is Hitler the go to reference for people when they want to symbolize the president as an awful person?

- When Bush was president I heard all the anti-Bush jokes and stories. How come I have not heard any anti-Obama stories or quotes prior to this book?

OBAMA DERANGEMENT SYNDROME

Obama is Hitler. Obama is a Communist. Obama is Muslim. Obama is not a citizen. Obama is the Antichrist.

If you agree with any or all of these statements, go see a doctor. You might be suffering from Obama Derangement Syndrome—pathological hatred of the president often mistaken for healthy patriotism.

It's a hydra-headed hysteria—cut off one accusation and another emerges in its place. The condition is apparently contagious, communicable through a steady diet of hyper-partisan talk radio and Wingnut Web sites. Its ugliest manifestation has led some to call—and even pray—for the death of the president. The fury of Obama Derangement Syndrome's emergence shocked even the most jaded political observers.

The day after Election 2008 ended, the Obama resistance began. The Drudge Report had been featuring ominous black-and-white photos of candidate Obama on its popular home page for days. Now banner ads on the site announced the beginning of an organized "Patriotic, Resilient, Conservative Resistance" to the president-elect at the Grassfire Nation Web site, bridging the ugliest rhetoric of the campaign with what would erupt in the Tea Party protests and town halls.

Wealth redistribution and higher taxes? We Resist! Government takeover of more and more of our lives? We Resist! Open borders, amnesty and undermining of our uniquely American culture? We Resist! Taxpayer-funded abortions and a radical anti-life agenda? We Resist! The weakening of our military and retreat in the war on Terror? We Resist! Socialized health care? We Resist! The end of marriage and the exaltation of LGBT rights? We Resist! International taxation and submitting our nation to the ideals of "global citizenship"? We Resist! The Courts stacked with leftist judges who betray our Constitution? We Resist![1]

Obama's opponents were already invested in a nightmare vision of the future, a far-left socialist dystopia opposed only by a small band of militant patriots. This fear-based appeal drew half a million visitors in its first month online and succeeded in registering a quarter million people before Inauguration Day.[2]

The word "resistance" is loaded with history: It was invoked by white opposition to Reconstruction after the Civil War, it was reborn as an organized policy of "massive resistance" during the southern desegregation battles a century later and more recent militia movements proclaim the virtues of armed "leaderless resistance." But this call to arms was relatively civil compared to the raw expressions of hate incubated down at the netroots.

Only minutes after the election, a death threat was posted to the Fox News Web site FoxForum—"Let's have a huge parade . . . How about Nov 22 . . . in Dallas . . . Barack can ride in the back of a convertible with his wife . . . they could drive by the School Book Depository."[3]

Over at fringe Web site American Sentinel, an unhinged culture warrior named Michael Eden fired off his own welcome to the White House: "Barack Hussein Obama and his Democratic lackeys get to wear the bull's-eyes on their foreheads for the duration of the next election cycle . . . don't let a bunch of appallingly blatant hypocrites tell you that you owe Obama one more iota of respect than they gave Bush . . . It's time to start burning down their houses and salting their fields."[4]

A white supremacist Web site, Stormfront, founded by a former Grand Dragon of the Ku Klux Klan, reported 2,800 new users in the first twenty-four hours after the election.[5] One poster on the site—identified as Dalderian Germanicus of North Las Vegas—wrote, "I want the SOB laid out in a box to see how 'messiahs' come to rest. God has abandoned us, this country is doomed."[6]

The crazy extended right into the halls of Congress. It was a Republican from Georgia named Paul Broun who got first dibs on the post-election comparisons of Obama to Hitler and Soviet dictators. In an interview with the AP, Broun referenced Obama's proposal for a civilian reserve corps—an idea endorsed by the Bush administration to handle postwar reconstruction efforts, but which had become a fearful talking point on the far right with

first Hitler comparison

Obama in power. "That's exactly what Hitler did in Nazi Germany and it's exactly what the Soviet Union did," Broun said. "When he's proposing to have a national security force that's answering to him, that is as strong as the U.S. military, he's showing me signs of being Marxist." Broun clarified his statement by saying, "We can't be lulled into complacency. You have to remember that Adolf Hitler was elected in a democratic Germany."[7] Broun's office refused to issue an apology.

Even churches couldn't offer safe harbor. The Sunday after the election, the Rev. Jay Scott Newman told his South Carolina parishioners they should not take communion if they voted for "Barack Hussein Obama" because "our nation has chosen for its chief executive the most radical pro-abortion politician ever to serve in the United States Senate or to run for president" and that "constitutes material cooperation with intrinsic evil."[8]

It might be tempting to dismiss these statements as the work of a few well-placed cranks, congressmen and clergy. But the Secret Service reported more threats against Obama than any other president-elect.[9] The politics of hate has a trickle-down effect, as the residents of Madison County, Idaho—which voted 85 percent for McCain-Palin—found out days after the election when a schoolbus full of second- and third-graders chanted "assassinate Obama."[10]

All these incidents occurred in the week after the election—so much for a presidential honeymoon.

Praying for the President's Death

"I hate Barack Obama. You say, well, you just mean you don't like what he stands for. No, I hate the person. Oh, you mean you just don't like his policies. No, I hate him . . . I am not going to pray for his good. I am going to pray that he dies and goes to hell."[11]

Here endeth the lesson at the Faithful Word Baptist Church in Tempe, Arizona. That's where Pastor Steven L. Anderson fired off a straight-to-the-point sermon on Sunday, August 16, 2009, titled "Why I Hate Barack Obama."

"Obama is overturning the U.S. Constitution, overturning everything we believe as a country, overturning some 200 years of history," Anderson thundered from the pulpit. "He is the revolutionary and it's a socialist/communist revolution. We are the counter-revolutionaries saying no, we don't want a change." He even offered parishioners a view into his own private Obama prayer: "Break his teeth, oh God, in his mouth; as a snail which melteth, let him pass away; like an untimely birth of a woman—that he thinks—he calls it a woman's right to choose, you know, he thinks it's so wonderful, he ought to be aborted. It ought to be, 'Abort Obama,' that ought to be the motto."[12]

Anderson can be dismissed as a deranged fringe figure, Elmer Gantry on a hate bender. Pastor Wiley Drake over in Orange County, California, is a more troubling phenomenon. He served as a second vice president of the Southern Baptist Convention in 2006 and 2007. In

2008, he received 47,000 votes as the vice presidential nominee of the American Independent Party, alongside conservative activist Alan Keyes. But that's not what he's best known for these days.

Pastor Drake first surfaced on the national political radar when he declared that the death of Kansas abortionist George Tiller—murdered in church on May 31, 2009—occurred because he had prayed for it. "George Tiller was far greater in his atrocities than Adolf Hitler," Drake told Fox's Alan Colmes, "so I am happy. I am glad that he is dead." Then he took a deeper leap into infamy by calmly announcing that he was also offering imprecatory prayers for the death of "the usurper that is in the White House . . . B. Hussein Obama."[13]

I wanted to see what a man who prays for the president's death is like in person, so I arranged to meet him on his home turf. The encounter provided a surprising portrait of someone living with a full-blown case of Obama Derangement Syndrome.

Drake's First Southern Baptist Church stands less than a mile from an amusement park, Knott's Berry Farm, in Orange County. It's a beige cinderblock building constructed in the 1950s. In its front yard, a broken wooden set of Ten Commandments juts out of a rock. A sign reading "ETERNITY" hangs over a flickering Coke machine.

Out back, a genial gray-haired man greets me, looking every inch the western grandfather of five. He's wearing a red shirt with black suspenders and a senior citizen—friendly big-buttoned cell phone hung on a string around his neck. This is the man who is praying for President Obama's death.

Wiley ushers me back into the empty church, past a sign saying "God Bless America," and we sit in the front pew. Hard-core haters are rarely friendly, their lives rarely fascinating, tending instead toward bitter isolation. But Wiley Drake's life story, it turns out, has a Forrest Gump quality.

Wiley at thirteen, shouting as nine African-American students are escorted by armed U.S. soldiers into a Little Rock, Arkansas, school: "2-4-8 we're not gonna integrate!" ("I grew up with the prejudice like everybody else did and thought I was right for a number of years," he says regretfully.) Wiley at eighteen, on the USS *Kitty Hawk* when the captain said on the loudspeaker, "We've been ordered to go to the South China Sea and to furnish air support for what's going on in a place called Indochina."

The late sixties found Wiley married and ministering to the poor at the Union Rescue Mission in downtown Los Angeles and to Jesus Freak hippies on Huntington Beach. Incongruously, he also joined the John Birch Society and got a degree in communications from the University of Southern California. A brief stint in the private sector working for global manufacturing conglomerate Ingersoll Rand found Wiley at the U.S. Embassy in Iran days before the gates were stormed and hostages taken. He was already souring on his fellow

Southern Baptist in the White House. "Carter began to have cocktails in the White House, and that to me was a dead giveaway," Wiley sniffs. "He wasn't as strict as he thought he was."

Back in Arkansas and back in the church, Wiley was part of a group of pastors approached by Bill Clinton as he tried to regain the governor's mansion in 1982. "He said, 'I lost because I didn't have the support of the church,' and he said, 'I want to put morality back in the governor's mansion.' . . . I said, 'Hey, this guy sounds good.' So I literally helped Bill Clinton get re-elected as the Comeback Kid. I very quickly found out that I had been flimflammed and sold a bill of goods; so then it was my desire to come back to Southern California."

Like many a fundamentalist, Wiley is a biblical literalist with a fondness for the Old Testament: "Just because man changed the law doesn't mean God's law is changed," he explains. "The Bible says that if a man lays down with a man, or a woman with a woman, it deserves death—and that's why the average homosexual only lives about less than 50 years of age on either side, man or woman. And now we're being told that we can't preach the Bible and that if we do it's a hate crime." This is the Right-Wingnut's vision of Big Brother—a liberal oppressor in conflict with God's law.

But strict readings of the Old Testament have been used to justify slavery and segregation from pulpits in the past. Where would Wiley draw the line today? "Do you believe then that disobedient children should be stoned, like it says in the Old Testament?" I asked. Wiley hesitated and chose his words carefully. "Yes, I believe that if a child is continuing to be totally disobedient, totally reprobate, then stoning would be biblically correct and legally correct."

As Wiley sees it, his devotion to speaking the word of God is what's caused all this controversy. "I'm known as a Birther, you know. I don't believe Obama was born in this country. He's an illegal alien and so forth. And so I began to pray what the Bible teaches us to pray and that is imprecatory prayer.

"An imprecatory prayer is very strong. Imprecatory prayer in Psalms 109 for example says if you have an evil leader above you, you pray that Satan will stand by his side and you ask God to make his children fatherless and his wife a widow and that his time in office be short . . . Other psalms say when they speak evil, God will break out their teeth and when they run to do destruction, God will break their legs."

To those offended by the idea of praying for death, Wiley shrugs. "I'm praying the word of God. I didn't write it. Don't get mad at me." But threatening the president's life is a felony, and when word got out about Wiley's imprecatory prayers he says the feds came over for a visit. "Within a week I had Secret Service people knocking on my door at the house saying we want to talk to you. And I said no; I'm not talking to you. I don't have to talk to you. I have freedom of speech. You want to talk to me, see my attorney."

After the election, Wiley became one of the first to file a lawsuit alleging that Obama was constitutionally ineligible for office because he was born not in the United States but Kenya. Drake says that Obama had been on his radar even before the campaign. "When he was still in Chicago, I had heard that the Communist Party had chosen him to be the one that they would bring about in this nation. I heard a testimony of a businessman who had been at a meeting overseas where they said, 'We're gonna bring a man to America that's going to be the next president and he's gonna be coming from Africa' and so forth. They said, 'In fact, we even know his name—Barack.' So I had heard early on that he was the proverbial Manchurian candidate."

And what do you think will happen to America if Barack Obama is in office for a full two terms?

"I think most preachers like me are going to be in jail," says Wiley. "I don't know if you're familiar with H.R. 645, but it is the bill to set up at least a half a dozen encampments around the country, and one of the reasons . . . is to have a place to intern those that are faith-based organizations."

"Where do you get your information?" I ask.

"Well, the Internet, of course . . . WorldNetDaily is one of my favorite Web sites."

Having hit the Manchurian candidate and government plans for concentration camps in short order, I decided to go down the Obama Derangement Syndrome checklist with Wiley.

"Do you believe Obama's a Muslim?"

"Oh absolutely. No doubt about it. No doubt in my mind he's a Muslim . . . he sort of likes Christianity, but he is primarily a Muslim." Check.

Next. "Some people call him Hitler or call him a communist. They use words like 'treason' or 'traitor.'"

"Well, those are all terms in my opinion that fit," says Wiley. "If you look at how Hitler used children, he came up with the whole idea of kindergarten to brainwash the children. And Obama has come up with this whole concept of getting the children to chant and to literally worship him. He's followed Alinsky and others. He's very much following their pattern: to take over the country, to take us down economically. He knows that if he can take us down economically, then when the people are poor, the people will follow almost anyone, anyone that holds out any hope."

One final question: "Do you think that Barack Obama is the Antichrist?"

Wiley sighed and furrowed his brow. "In my opinion, and my theological understanding of the Scripture, there will be one last days, in the last days there will be one Antichrist, but there will be several that lead up to the Antichrist, and I'm of the opinion that Barack Hussein Obama is the Antichrist."

"How exactly?"

"Well, you know, in reference to the fact that the Antichrist will be the one that's going to want to be the savior of the world, not through Jesus or God, but *being* the savior [himself]. We have to have medical care for everybody. We have to have all of these bailouts—control and own and operate. He has come as close to an Antichrist as anybody ever has in this country because, you know, it's not General Motors anymore. It's Government Motors. And he's taken over the banks and he's taken over everything."

So, to be clear, you believe that President Obama is going to bring about the end of the world?

"Absolutely, yeah. I don't have any idea how and when. But I think there's going to be some resistance . . . We're just seeing a resistance movement. We're seeing a group of people that are saying, 'Enough is enough. We're not going to let Congress do this.'"

The prospect of a cleansing Armageddon is pleasing to this grandfather of five. "People are finally waking up. One of the things that the Bible indicates about the Antichrist is that he will force the issues so much so that there will indeed be one last big war. And I think we're headed for that war."

How Obama Became Hitler, a Communist and the Antichrist

You never forget your first Obama-is-the-Antichrist e-mail. Mine came in July 2008, with the subject header "This Should Open Our Eyes." What opened my eyes most was that it was sent sincerely by a generally sane local attorney and family friend. We've had presidents called Hitler, a Communist and even the Antichrist in the past, but no president before Obama has hit the full insanity trifecta so fast. Which got me wondering: How did this happen?

In search of answers, I wandered through the Wingnutsphere and found out how these contradictory conspiracy theories took flight from the fringe to mainstream consciousness—from e-mails and talk radio to cable news and then a protest near you. It shows the evolution of an idea, a genealogy of hate and hyperpartisanship in our time.

Obama as Hitler

Godwin's Law states that the longer any online debate goes on, the likelier it is that someone will play the Nazi card. It's the rhetorical equivalent of going nuclear and stupid at the same time. It used to be the reflexive attack of the campus politically correct crowd on conservatives, but in Obama's first year a political role reversal was pulled off—Hitler was now a liberal.

This was a neat trick, inspired in part by a popular and thoughtful anti–big government treatise by *National Review* editor-at-large Jonah Goldberg (and son of Clinton nemesis Lucianne Goldberg), titled "Liberal Fascism." It allowed conservatives to de-link the right with fascism by pointing out that Nazis got their name because they were national socialists. Goldberg himself pointed to an overlap in Obama's utopian rhetoric on

Glenn Beck's show during the spring of '08: "When Barack Obama campaigns, he's basically saying, 'I'm a silver bullet. I'm going to solve all your problems just by electing me.' FDR, Hitler, all these guys, they basically said, 'All your problems can be solved.'"[14]

The initial point of departure wasn't dictatorship or genocide but the ugliest imaginable partisan spin on Obama's oratorical talents. It's an interesting move: You turn inspiration into adulation and then you call it a cult of personality—next stop, Hitler.

The first known Obama-Hitler comparison occurred in February 2008, when Fox News radio host Tom Sullivan offered side-by-side airings of Obama's speech at the Iowa Jefferson-Jackson dinner and a Hitler speech.[15] After Obama's address in Germany outside the Brandenburg Gate, conservative columnist Charles Krauthammer drily made the same point: "Standing in front of 200,000 Germans at a rally who are chanting your name—Bad vibes sometimes, historically."[16] "Seventy-five-thousand people at an outdoor sports palace, well, that's something the Führer would have done," concurred conservative economist (and sometime actor—". . . *Bueller? Bueller?*") Ben Stein after Obama's August nomination acceptance speech at Denver's Invesco Field at Mile High.[17] Ann Coulter reached for another form of literary comparison, casting "B. Hussein's" memoir *Dreams from My Father* as "a dime store *Mein Kampf.*"[18]

Soon the comparison started gaining currency at the grassroots. A sign drawn up by a volunteer in one of the

McCain campaign's Florida field offices compared "Barack Hussein Obama" to a litany of dictators from Hitler to Stalin to Mussolini to Castro. "Who else called for change in this fashion?" the sign asked. "Each and every one called on youth movements. And you want Obama for President? Are you nuts!"[19]

The designer of the sign, a self-identified "12th-generation" American named Robert E. J. Driscoll was dismissed from volunteering for the campaign but refused to apologize. He said he had been offended by the way activists on the left had compared Bush to Hitler without mainstream media criticism. In any case, he told the *Sun-Sentinel,* "Clinically and morally there is nothing wrong with the poster. . . . If I compare the oration ability of Senator Obama with that of Adolf Hitler (both quite good in communicating), does that mean I am suggesting Obama will be a mass murderer? Of course not."[20]

Congressman Paul Broun's post-election outburst comparing Obama to Hitler offered a similar qualification: "I'm not comparing him to Adolf Hitler. What I'm saying is there is the potential of going down that road."[21]

The delicate politics of this differentiation was explained in fuller detail by the master of political-attack-as-entertainment, Rush Limbaugh: "When you're dealing with a guy like Obama and the Democrat Party, who are going to impose Nazi-like socialism policies on this country, you've got to say it. And the same time you say it, you have to go out and point we're not talking about the genocide—that's at the tail end of Hitler."[22]

Right. So the Wingnut argument is that they are not comparing Obama to Hitler the genocidal dictator, but they're comparing Obama to Hitler the political leader—those six million Jews murdered in the Holocaust are just a detail people keep getting hung up on.

In April '09, as the Republican Party's officials tried to regroup, Michigan party chair Saul Anuzis—an ambitious if unsuccessful aspirant for national RNC Chair—advanced the ball by advising the GOP to characterize Obama's policies as "economic fascism." "We've so overused the word 'socialism' that it no longer has the negative connotation it had 20 years ago, or even 10 years ago," Anuzis reasoned. "Fascism—everybody still thinks that's a bad thing."[23]

Later that month, Glenn Beck obligingly picked up the talking point: "They're marching us to a non-violent fascism. Or to put it another way, they're marching us to 1984. Big Brother. Like it or not, fascism is on the rise."[24] Fox producers partnered the commentary with a minute's worth of goose-stepping Nazi b-roll.

The message was received loud and clear. In June, the president of the Republican Women of Anne Arundel County, Maryland, fired off this e-mail complete with the requisite paranoid capital letters: "Obama and Hitler have a great deal in common in my view. Obama and Hitler use the 'blitzkrieg' method to overwhelm their enemies. FAST, CARPET BOMBING intent on destruction.

Hitler's blitzkrieg bombing destroyed many European cities—quickly and effectively. Obama is systematically destroying the American economy and with it AMERICA."[25]

Prefab Obama-as-Hitler signs began to pop up at August health-care town halls, featuring the president with a narrow mustache, bearing the slogan: "I've changed." They were the product of the conspiracy theory cult of Lyndon LaRouche. It was a LaRouche aide named Anton Chaitkin who started the Obama-as-Hitler attack on healthcare in response to what he called "a propaganda movement for euthanasia." Soon pamphlets were produced: "Act Now to Stop Obama's Nazi Health Plan!"

In Massachusetts, Congressman Barney Frank's town hall was disrupted by a glassy-eyed young LaRouche-ite who asked, "Why are you supporting this Nazi policy, as Obama has?" (Frank deserves bipartisan props for his response: "On what planet do you spend most of your time?")

In Nevada, at a Las Vegas town hall, an Israeli-American was defending Israel's national health care to reporters when a woman named Pamela Pigler shouted, "Heil Hitler!" and then proceeded to make whining sounds mocking him when he took offense. Pigler later explained, "I'm a conservative and I just believe in biblical values."[26] It remains unclear how shouting "Heil Hitler" is consistent with biblical values.

In Iowa, a World War II vet named Tom Eisenhower (presumably no relation to the late president) proclaimed to the crowd at Senator Chuck Grassley's town hall, "The president of the United States, that's who you should be concerned about. Because he's acting like a little Hitler. . . . I'd take a gun to Washington if enough of you would go with me."[27]

By the 9/12 march on Washington, dozens of homemade Obama-as-Hitler signs were a prominent part of the scenery. I saw side-by-side portraits of the president next to Hitler and Lenin, with the tag, "In troubled times the fearful and naïve are always drawn to charismatic radicals. We will never allow this Change to happen." There was iconic Nazi-era imagery with President Obama pasted in as "the new face of national socialism."

The seeds of the association had blossomed into fullfledged acceptance by some people on Main Street. An Ohio couple didn't understand why they were denied a permit to drive through the annual Fredricktown Tomato Show Parade on a float that showed President Obama with a swastika armband beside a Nazi flag.[28] Richard and Jacqueline Ruhl said they found "strong parallels between what President Obama is doing and Adolf Hitler" and proposed the float as a way to get their neighbors to "wake up."

"It was the swastikas that seemed to be turning off most people," reflected Jackie. "We are not extremists and we have not done anything like this before. . . . He denied us our First Amendment right. He is an extremist," Jackie said, referring to President Obama. "If anyone thinks I like pulling a swastika around, they are crazy," said Richard. "I hated it just as much as any-body."[29]

With the growing use of the Obama-as-Hitler compar-ison, a few more GOP leaders started indulging as well.

Former Bush administration official Ellen Sauer-brey—who served as assistant secretary of state and was a two-time GOP nominee for governor in Maryland—reportedly told a September Lincoln/Reagan dinner audience that the president was surrounded by "a cult-like following edging toward those of past dictators like Juan Perón and even Adolf Hitler."[30] When subse-quently asked to clarify her comments by the *County Times,* Sauerbrey denied having dropped the H-bomb but acknowledged: "I think that we have a government that is following policies that are socialistic and fascist."[31]

Georgia Congressman John Linder, a member of the powerful House Ways and Means Committee, decided to make his Hitler comparisons in op-ed form, penning a condemnation of progressivism for Politico that tied to-gether Robespierre, Woodrow Wilson, Hitler, Mussolini and Obama: "All believed in the minimum wage, state control of private property for the public good, union-ization and environmentalism. And they believed in eu-genics to purify the gene pool."[32]

All these Nazi comparisons made me wonder what ac-tual Nazis thought of the hype—it must be bittersweet for them to have the first African-American president referred to as Hitler, a curious mix of pride and prejudice. I hunted down the phone number of the northeast Nazi chapter (apparently, they are fussy about being called the American National Socialist Party) and got someone who called himself SS Corporal Schneider on the line.

"The people who are referring to him as a Nazi know very little or nothing about authentic Nazi-ism," Schneider stiffly said. "I'd laugh if it wasn't so ludicrous. The last thing in the world I would ever call President Obama—and I hesitate to call him president—is a Nazi. I most certainly would not refer to him as a Nazi. It seems to me that if he was successful at what he was doing, he'd be more of a communist than a Nazi. A Nazi is completely at the opposite end of the spectrum where he is concerned . . . and his is not a Nazi health plan, not by any stretch of the imagination." So we've got that creepily cleared up.

I couldn't resist pressing Schneider on how self-styled Aryans feel about the Obama comparisons: "Having the first African-American president being the one who's been called Nazi the most—that's got to get under your skin."

"Well, you'll find no blacks among the ranks of the National Socialist movement, for obvious reasons," Schneider understated. "It gets under members' skin, not so much because of his color, but because of his ideas and some of the things that he's been saying. . . . The concept of color in the movement here is not quite the issue that it was."

In Schneider's world, the Nazi party is "comprised of taxpaying, law abiding, nine-to-five working people who are very devoted to their families, pay their taxes, stop for red lights, respect the police and the law and basically are out to support their own country and save it from the ruination of the corrupt politicians that are destroying and undermining this entire system." But are there any politicians he likes? "Reagan. And if that man came back from the dead, I'd vote for him again. It's just a shame that the man passed away and it's just a shame that man couldn't have been president for life."

Perhaps the best response to all this Wingnut distortion of history came from one seventy-year-old man, a classically trained musician by the name of Henry Gasparian. His family had experienced real Nazis—not metaphorical ones—in Armenia during the Second World War.

They'd killed his uncles and sent a cousin to die in a concentration camp. When he saw the Obama-as-Hitler posters at a sidewalk protest near his home in Seattle, his reaction was "personal and emotional." A heated conversation turned into a shoving match, and the cops came and took Gasparian away. His son, who bailed him out of jail eight hours later, was shocked, saying his father had never received more than a speeding ticket. But Henry was unrepentant. "I saw Hitler's soldiers. I saw swastikas every day," he said. "To call Obama stupid, even criminal—okay, that's politics. But Hitler? It's hurting to anyone no matter who is president."[33]

Obama as Communist

"There is no doubt that he is a Marxist, but he is much more than that, much more dangerous than that—and this is the reality that should make all Americans very very nervous and fearful."[34]

No, it's not Barack Obama they're referring to. It's Bill Clinton being called a Marxist Manchurian candidate back in the 1990s.

The same Wingnut Web site, WorldNetDaily, has been pushing the same paranoid argument against President Obama complete with epic pre-election screeds with titles like "Barack Obama *really is* a Manchurian Candidate."[35] (I love the "*really*"—in their italics. It's vaguely apologetic in a boy-who-cried-wolf sort of way—they might have been wrong about Bubba, but they've got the real Marxist Manchurian candidate this time.)

The slippery slope from socialist to communist attacks on Obama began during the campaign. It focused first on economics. When Barack Obama met "Joe the Plumber" in Toledo, Ohio, and uttered the phrase "spread the wealth," socialism became an omnipresent Hail Mary campaign tactic. Sarah Palin enthusiastically dove in, repeatedly saying, "Now is no time to experiment with socialism."[36]

Former Republican House Majority leader Tom DeLay hammered home the theme a bit harder: "Unless he proves me wrong, he is a Marxist."[37] On CNN's *Larry King Live,* conservative radio show host Lars Larson recommended that McCain needed "to tag Obama as the Marxist that he is."[38]

But for most conservatives, calling Obama an outright communist seemed a stretch. The defamatory door was opened with examinations of his family history. Writing on National Review Online, former Dan Quayle speechwriter[39] Lisa Schriffen wondered whether Obama's parents had first met through a love of communism: "How had these two come together at a time when it was neither natural nor easy for such relationships to flourish? Always through politics. No, not the young Republicans. Usually the Communist Youth League. Or maybe a different arm of the CPUSA. But, for a white woman to marry a black man in 1958, or 60, there was almost inevitably a connection to explicit Communist politics."[40]

Allegations of Obama's influence under "communist and socialist mentors" while growing up in Hawaii and later Chicago occupied a chapter in the best-selling *Obama Nation: Leftist Politics and the Cult of Personality*. Written by WorldNetDaily senior staff reporter Jerome R. Corsi, author of the anti–John Kerry tome *Unfit for Command*, the book concluded that Obama "is a likely communist sympathizer."

Down the stretch, Ohio-based conservative radio host Bill Cunningham went into full communist-revolution-is-coming mode, telling his 200,000 swing-state listeners, "Much like Castro took over Cuba, Mao Zedong took over Red China, and the Communists took over Russia, Obama now is poised—according to many of my good friends on the left . . . to seize power in America, and I hope [it will] be a bloodless coup."[41]

Shortly after the election, Michael Savage managed to tie the communist and birther crazy all together for his audience. "We're getting ready for the Communist takeover of America with a non-citizen at the helm—I love it."[42]

All this remained festering on the fringes, until Glenn Beck's new show debuted on Fox in January. Sixteen days into the new administration, Beck featured a graphic showing America galloping down the road from capitalism to socialism and then to communism—and then began offering a regular "Comrade Update."[43]

At the Tax Day Tea Party in '09, Obama-as-communist signs first started to pop up in the crowd, next to the protestations of patriotism and fidelity to the Founding Fathers. At the City Hall Park rally in New York, I went up to one guy impassively holding a giant placard that read "Hussein = Commie." He was wearing a hoodie and sunglasses and holding an iPod—a hipster irony outfit by way of the Unibomber—so I asked him if the sign was serious. Oh, yeah.

"Every time he opens his mouth he spouts textbook Marxism, communism, socialism," said the man who initially gave his name as "Barry Soetoro"—Obama's name when he lived in Indonesia as a child. After some prodding, it turned out the protester was a Manhattan real estate executive with a degree in economics from Georgetown. This was a high end kind of crazy.

Likewise, Alan Keyes has a pedigree that would seem to counter off-the-rails accusations. But Keyes can be considered patient zero in the spread of Obama Derangement Syndrome. The one-time protégé of Reagan's U.N. ambassador, Jeane Kirkpatrick, and three-time presidential candidate was recruited to run against then State Senator Barack Obama in 2004 for the Illinois U.S. Senate seat, despite the fact that Keyes lived in Maryland. (That the GOP could not find an African-American candidate to run in all of Illinois, the Land of Lincoln, is its own evidence of the Party of Lincoln's problems.) In his 2006 book, *The Audacity of Hope,* Obama angrily recounts Keyes's campaign claim that "Christ would not vote for Barack Obama."

Keyes has only ratcheted up his rhetoric since then, both in his 2008 third-party campaign for the presidency alongside Wiley Drake and in comments outside a Nebraska anti-abortion fund-raiser in the spring of 2009. "Obama is a radical communist, and I think it is becoming clear. That is what I told people in Illinois and now everybody realizes it's true," Keyes told a reporter from local station KHAS-TV. "He is going to destroy this country, and we are either going to stop him or the United States of America is going to cease to exist."[44]

By the summer of 2009, the Soviet hammer and sickle was being slapped on e-mails and T-shirts, advertised by smiling girls on conservative Web sites, purchasable on bumper stickers, tote bags and mugs. Search online for "Obama" and "communist" or "hammer and sickle" and hundreds of Internet images pop up. The proliferation of Obama-as-communist gear is presumably supposed to be sarcastic opposition or ironic commentary—the on-line retailer Noisebot.com actually labeled one of its wares as a "funny Obama communist T-shirt."

Twenty years after the end of the Cold War, I can appreciate how easy it is to treat communism as a curiosity, like the last Japanese soldier found wanting to fight for the Emperor on a Pacific island in 1974. But any ideology that managed to murder 100 million people in less than a century is not a joke. It's a conduit for evil.

At the 9/12 march on Washington, there were posters of Obama as Che Guevara over the slogan "Obamunism." There were signs telling America to "Wake Up" with pictures of Obama alongside Lenin and Castro, while another featured Obama's face morphing into Stalin's. Obama was painted as the Joker in white face and lipstick over the slogan "I lied" and "Communism isn't funny." One veteran held a sign that read, "I didn't serve in the military to live in a socialist country" and "Obama's America looks a lot like the Soviet Union." Another proclaimed "Red Dawn 2009: The Enemy is Within."

A glossy poster of Joe McCarthy holding a photo of Obama caught my eye. "Vindicated," it read. Its creator was a twenty-four-year-old from Pennsylvania named Brad. "When I was younger, I always heard right-wing speech from my grandfather about Joseph McCarthy and the communists," he said. "But now you come to

realize that there are a lot of socialists not only in Hollywood but in the public school systems, and they've
taken over the media and sort of hijacked democracy, so
I figured this was good."

I went up to one woman dressed as a cross between
Betsy Ross and Mrs. Claus and asked her what message
she was trying to send.

"I was in Cuba at the age of twelve when Castro took
over," she said. "He promised a change just like this
president is promising us, and right after that he began
to do certain things that I see very familiar now, the
same steps toward total control. So I had no choice but
to leave my country as a child without my parents. . . . I
never saw them again, and here I am fifty years later
with concern that our children here might run into the
same problems that we had."

So do you really think there are parallels between
Castro and Obama? I asked. "Yes," she said. "Do some
reading and you'll see. Go to the Communist Party
U.S.A."

So I did.

"Obama is certainly no communist," Communist
Party U.S.A. national board member Dan Margolis told
me. "There's no way that you could say that he's gone
anywhere close to being a communist. The only similar-
ity I can see is that Fidel Castro said the word 'change'
and Obama uses the word 'change.' . . . The idea that
Obama is somehow leading a socialist revolution in this

country is just patently ridiculous. Actually, I don't even see any parallels."

"His policies aren't socialist," Comrade Margolis insisted. "You know, with the economic crisis, they wanted to prop up big finance. What we would have said is simply: 'We need to nationalize these banks.' . . . We're not happy with the idea of escalating troops in Afghanistan. We don't see a military victory there as really possible. . . . And health care, of course, if it were up to us we'd have socialized medicine."

But wait, isn't the whole debate over whether Obama's health-care plan constitutes socialized medicine? "It's clearly not socialized medicine," said Margolis. "An example of socialized medicine would be Cuba, where all doctors are employees of the government. . . . We consider that a better system but that's not what Obama's proposing." It turns out that Obama wasn't even the Democratic candidate communists saw as the closest thing to a fellow traveler in the '08 campaign. The Communists liked Dennis Kucinich.

Obama as Antichrist

Twenty-five percent of Americans have heard the rumor that Obama is the Antichrist (the biblically predicted false messiah who will rule the world until the second coming of Christ), according to a Scripps-Howard poll.[45] This is courtesy of a widely circulated e-mail chain that began to hit critical mass in March 2008, when Obama was on the verge of clinching the nomination:

> According to The Book of Revelations [sic] . . . the Anti-Christ will be a man, in his 40s, of MUSLIM descent, who will deceive the nations with persuasive language, and have a MASSIVE Christ-like appeal. . . . the prophecy says that people will flock to him and he will promise false hope and world peace, and when he is in power, he will destroy everything.
>
> And Now: For the award winning Act of Stupidity Of all times the People of America want to elect, to the most Powerful position on the face of the Planet—The Presidency of the United States of America . . . A Muslim Male Extremist Between the ages of 17 and 40.
>
> Have the American People completely lost their Minds, or just their Power of Reason ???
>
> I'm sorry but I refuse to take a chance on the "unknown" candidate Obama.

The e-mail was a small classic in paranoid politics and character assassination, bringing together war-on-terror anxiety, the moral authority of religious imagery and McCain campaign talking points about "the unknown Obama."

Among the folks who forwarded the e-mail was Mayor Danny Funderburk of Fort Mill, South Carolina, who explained to an inquiring reporter, "I was just curious if there was any validity to it. . . . I was trying to get documentation if there was any Scripture to back it up."[46]

Former *Saturday Night Live* comedienne turned conservative blogger Victoria Jackson also jumped in, writing that Obama "bears traits that resemble the anti-Christ."[47]

I met more believers in this theory in the summer of 2009, when Shirley Phelps-Roper decided to take her two young daughters on a field trip from Topeka, Kansas to Manhattan. They were coming to celebrate—yes, celebrate—the death of Walter Cronkite outside his memorial service.

You might have heard of the Phelps-Roper family from the Westboro Baptist Church because of their practice of protesting at soldiers' funerals—where signs range from "God Hates Fags" to "God Hates America"—apparently because we don't hate quite enough for their taste. I ran into them on a bright Tuesday morning on the Upper West Side, where they were killing time in a pre-game protest outside a Jewish community center, stomping on American and Israeli flags. The daughters Megan and Grace were carrying signs that read "Barack Obama is the anti-Christ" and "America is Doomed."

I asked what Megan thought of President Obama. Her eyes lit up. "Oh, he's the Antichrist," she said. I ask for a little more explanation. "Well, he's against Christ," she said.

Liberty University Law School Dean Matthew Staver felt he had to offer a word of caution to those who wanted to go the full crazy: While he did not personally believe Obama is the Antichrist, he could see how others might. "They are expressing a concern and a fear that is widely shared."[48] Depressingly, the journalistic accuracy site Snopes found it necessary to burst these hot-air balloons, pointing out that "nothing in the Bible—in Revelation or elsewhere—describes the anti-Christ as being 'a man, in his 40s, of Muslim descent.' In fact, since the book of Revelation was complete by the end of the second century, but the religion of Islam wasn't founded until about 400 years later, the notion that Revelation would have mentioned the word 'Muslim' at all is rather far-fetched."[49]

Despite the chronological absurdity, the McCain campaign put out a Web ad that seemed to play on Obama-as-Antichrist fears. Titled "The One," it began with the sarcastic humor that distinguished the campaign's communication style, mocking Obama supporters' adulation of their candidate, interspersed with clips of Charlton Heston as Moses from Cecil B. DeMille's *The Ten Commandments*.

The ad careened off into scriptural wording—"And the world will receive his blessings"—and used imagery that recalled the cover of the 70-million-copies-selling *Left Behind* series which chronicles the rise of the Antichrist in politics. The Rev. Tim LaHaye, co-author of *Left Behind*, said he recognized allusions to his work in the ad.[50]

It was the creation of McCain media advisor Fred Davis, a man familiar with evangelical code as the friend of former Christian Coalition leader Ralph Reed and the nephew of conservative Oklahoma Senator James Inhofe. *Time* magazine editorialized, "It's not easy to make the infamous Willie Horton ad from the 1988 presidential campaign seem benign. But suggesting that Barack Obama is the Antichrist might just do it."[51]

The caricatures kept popping up, furthered by the mock humor/hysteria of partisan sites. WorldNetDaily repeatedly weighed in on the affirmative, while the conservative Web site RedState.com started selling T-shirts and mugs sporting a large "O" with horns and the words "The Anti-Christ" underneath.[52] Glenn Beck felt compelled to ask conservative evangelical leader Rev. John Hagee what were the "odds that Obama is the Antichrist?" Hagee said simply and clearly, "No Chance."[53]

The weekend before the election, the *Salt Lake Tribune* published an article addressing the fears: "For eons, Christians have believed the world is hurling toward oblivion. But with the current economic downturn, the war in Iraq and the likely election of Barack Obama, many think it has picked up speed."[54]

The so-called Rapture Index—an evangelical Web site that keeps tabs on signs that the end of the world may be at hand—reached 50,000 hits a day in the run-up to Election Day and the index hit new highs after Obama's election.[55]

And the Obama-as-Antichrist rumors didn't dissipate after the election; evangelicals were buzzing that the winning lottery numbers in Illinois the day after the election were 666, considered the biblical "mark of the beast." And in September 2009, Public Policy Polling found that 14 percent of New Jersey Republicans thought that Obama was the Antichrist, while 15 percent weren't sure. [56]

Look over all these disparate threads of Obama Derangement Syndrome—from comparisons to Hitler to communists to the Antichrist—and you'll see some common themes.

There is a recipe that keeps being repeated—a Wingnut claim that riffs on foundational fears is posted on a fringe Web site (usual suspects include WorldNetDaily or FreeRepublic) and then gets passed around. These dispatches from the outer limits get repeated on talk radio. They trickle down to the grassroots and appear on signs at protests. Eventually some elected official parrots the paranoia, playing to the base while venting their spleen. It makes news not only because the statements are outrageous but because they crystallize the crazy in our politics.

THE BIRTH OF
WHITE MINORITY POLITICS

There's one thing I can't help but notice every time I go to a Tea Party or a town hall, let alone the Republican national convention.

A *lot* of white people.

The crowds are weirdly monochromatic. Even in the heart of Washington, D.C., a city that is 55 percent African-American, I didn't see a single black person among the tens of thousands in the crowd at the 9/12 rally on the Washington Mall—it was a columnist's version of "Where's Waldo?"

Some liberals look at the opposition to Obama, and they can't wait to cry racism. Actress and activist Janeane Garofalo vented her spleen on behalf of many when she said, "This is about hating a black man in the White House. This is racism straight up. That is nothing but a bunch of teabagging rednecks."[1] Reflexively playing the race card may be emotionally satisfying for the left, but after covering the Tea Party protests and town halls up close, I don't believe simple racism is driving the opposition to President Obama. Yes, there is the drip drop of racist e-mails from small-town conservative officials and racially overtoned netroot nicknames for

Obama like "Ogabe" (a riff off Zimbabwe's dictator Robert Mugabe). Yes, American voting is still largely split on racial lines, and race has been a fundamental fault line in U.S. politics since the original sin of slavery. But as Barack Obama once pointed out, he was black before the election. His breakthrough caucus victory occurred in 96 percent white Iowa. America has come a long way from the brutal bigotry of the Bull Connor era.

Something more complex is going on.

We are witnessing the birth of white minority politics.

In some ways, it looks like the ethnic politics of past groups—like the millions of Irish or Italian immigrants who arrived annually at the turn of the last century—complete with the competing emotions of pride and victimization. There was a focus on preserving ancestral heritage against the onslaught of change in the new world. But this time the economic struggle isn't about climbing the ladder of success; it's about not falling further behind. With an increase of more than 2.2 million white males unemployed in the year since Obama's election,[2] they feel they are getting squeezed by a changing America—a bad economy combined with a slow-moving demographic tsunami.

They feel like a minority because they fear they are going to be a minority. The year 2050 has special resonance—that's the year that the U.S. census estimates whites will no longer be a majority in America.[3] In their eyes, Obama's election represents a new urban onslaught of educated minorities and immigrants who are pushing the rural whites who used to define what it meant to be an American down the economic food chain.

White minority politics is a politics of resistance to social change propelled by resentment. It resonates with people who feel like members of an oppressed minority, under siege by a modern multicultural America that is being imposed on them and disrespecting traditional American values in the process. It is an echo of what Richard Hofstadter described as a core characteristic of the paranoid style a half century ago: "America has been largely taken away from them and their kind, though they are determined to try to repossess it and to prevent the final destructive act of subversion."[4]

The signature rallying cry is "Take Our Country Back"—a slogan that surfaces at Tea Parties and town halls ("I want my country back, I don't want my flag to change!"). It is used on Wingnut Web sites, serves as a signature line on talk shows and provides the title for a conservative conference. (Coincidentally but perhaps not incidentally, the whites-only British National Party uses a similar slogan: "We Want Our Country Back.") It accompanies talk about the assault on American values and the undermining of our constitutional republic, of slavery via socialism, tyranny and totalitarianism. Rush Limbaugh tells his audience, "We're living in occupied territory. . . . We, the people of this country, need to be liberated. We are oppressed now."[5]

This desire to take the country back is combined with an idealized vision of America's past, a more pastoral time of small-town values and small government. It is unspoken that this was a largely white America. It's consistent with the way Confederate flags that occasionally wave in protest crowds are explained away by saying they represent "heritage, not hate." The appeal is so emotional that one sign I saw read simply, "Preserve Mom, Apple Pie and the American Way." In their eyes, the ideal of America is under assault.

Right-wing radio show host Michael Savage has been beating the drum of resistance and resentment hard. "In the past people would come over and become Americans. Now they come over and they want you to become them. They want you to speak Spanish, they want you to act Muslim, they want you to give up going to the church and go into a mosque," Savage said on August 20, 2009, as the town hall protests were erupting into occasional fistfights.

"We're gonna have a revolution in this country if this keeps up," Savage continued; "the rage has reached a boil. If they keep pushing us around and if we keep having these schmucks running for office catering to the multicultural people who are destroying the culture of this country, the white male—the one without connections, the one without money—has nothing to lose. . . . He is still the majority, no one speaks for him, everyone craps on him, people use him for cannon fodder, and he has no voice whatsoever. You're gonna find out that if you keep pushing this country around, there is an ugly side to the white male that has been suppressed for probably 30 years right now but it really has never gone away."[6]

It's not just the complaint of a few isolated shock jocks strutting their psychoses and doing the latest version of the angry white guy rant.

Conservative pundit and former Reagan communications director Pat Buchanan has been a prophet of white minority politics for decades, building a successful career on the concept from President Richard Nixon's southern strategy to his own pitchfork populist campaigns for the presidency. (While earning a reputation as a personally genial conservative voice on political talk shows, Pat Buchanan is not just an incidental advocate for these forces. His 2006 book, *State of Emergency,* was subtitled *The Third World Invasion and Conquest of America*. Buchanan has appeared twice on the avowedly white supremacist radio show *Political Cesspool,* most recently in July 2008. The host of *Political Cesspool,* James Edwards, attributes volunteering on Buchanan's 2000 presidential campaign to his political awakening.) Since Obama's election, Buchanan has been particularly prolific on the subject, writing about the plight of white voters: "America was once their country. They sense they are losing it. And they are right."[7]

Like Savage, but far more eloquent, Buchanan feels a forced cultural conversion is under way: "Without the assent of her people, America is being converted from a Christian country, nine in 10 of whose people traced their roots to Europe as late as the time of JFK, into a multiracial, multiethnic, multilingual, multicultural Tower of Babel not seen since the late Roman Empire."[8]

And Buchanan laments the new heroes of our evolving multicultural America: "Old heroes like Columbus, Stonewall Jackson, and Robert E. Lee are replaced by Dr. King and Cesar Chavez."[9]

The fact that Pat singled out not one but two members of the Confederate Army—including the now semi-obscure Jackson, whom southern Civil War historian Shelby Foote once described as having "a curious indifference to suffering"—speaks to the impulses behind this allegedly pro-America traditionalist movement.[10]

But a more popular metaphor than the defeated Confederacy is the founding of the United States, the American political scripture of the War of Independence.

Opposition to health-care reform was presented in online ads as a re-creation of the Continental Army's struggle against British tyranny, recast as a struggle for individual freedom against British-style big government health care. It's not a policy debate but a life-or-death fight for the soul of America, pitting conservatives against liberals, patriots against tyrants. The president's position is therefore fundamentally un-American.

This call provokes a response. At the 9/12 march, scattered among the crowd were dozens of folks who'd responded to an online call to wear Revolutionary War period garb, so as to make their deeper allegiance clear. The e-mail notice said reams about their hotbox loss of perspective:

Continental Soldiers Wanted for 9/12 March: Attention all
Revolutionary War re-enactors: arise, ye Patriots, to the
hallowed cause of liberty! If you have a Revolutionary-era
uniform—be it militia, frontiersman, rifleman, musician or
regular Continental Army—please bring it with you to the
9-12 march and be part of the Continental fife and drum
procession that will be leading the march. What better
way to send a message to those who would take away our
liberty than to remind them WE have not forgotten those
who sacrificed so much to give us our liberty.[11]

Beyond the odd enthusiasm for fife and drum re-
enactments, the broader point is one of fidelity to the
Founding Fathers' America. These marchers see themselves as defending America's heritage against a usurper
in the White House who wants to "take away our liberty." In their eyes, Obama doesn't understand the
national heritage because he's not part of it—he's an in-
ternationalist who grew up in Indonesia with the middle
name Hussein. He's not one of "us"— his administration
is called a "Thugocracy" or a "Gangster Government."
They point to the comment Michelle Obama made during the campaign—"For the first time in my adult life I
am proud of my country"—as evidence the president
doesn't take pride in our nation's history. He doesn't
share our heritage. He's not a real American.
Think back to the rapturous response Sarah Palin got
in what she called "real America." She debuted the divisive sound bite at a speech in Greensboro, North Carolina:

"We believe that the best of America is in these small towns that we get to visit, and in these wonderful little pockets of what I call the real America, being here with all of you hard working, very patriotic, very pro-America areas of this great nation."[12]

Of course, if "real America" is pro-American, than there is also a false America—by implication, the increasingly diverse and urban areas where most Americans now live—which is anti-American. This is an applause line for people staring into the political abyss.

Palin's "real America" riffs were not meant to be about race directly, but they applied almost exclusively to white small-town America.

Candidate Obama validated the fears of the emerging white minority—and the perception of him as an over-educated elitist—when he unwisely and unkindly disparaged the "bitter" working-class Americans of western Pennsylvania: "They cling to guns or religion or antipathy to people who aren't like them or anti-immigrant sentiment or anti-trade sentiment as a way to explain their frustrations."[13]

Unlike previous African-American presidential candidates, Obama rarely referred to his race on the campaign trail—he was determined not to run a protest candidacy like Jesse Jackson or Al Sharpton before him. He wasn't running to be the president of black America, he was running to be the president of the United States of America. But there were moments where the curtain came back on the role of race.

In Virginia, Bobbie May, the chairman of the Buchanan County McCain campaign, was forced to resign after he published an article in a local paper describing "The clarified platform of Barack Hussein Obama." It included the Second Amendment applying only to "gang-bangers" and "Islamo-fascist terrorists," "free drugs for Obama's inner city political base," "mandatory Black Liberation Theology courses taught in all churches" and hiring the rapper Ludacris to paint the White House black. The kicker predicted lines we've heard endlessly since: Obama wants to "change liberty and freedom to socialism and communism."[14]

Throughout the campaign there was the occasional racially overtoned vandalism of Obama field offices, and not infrequent outbursts from crowds. In eastern Ohio, news cameras caught flashes of unfiltered racial anxiety at a GOP rally, with one woman saying, "I'm afraid that if he wins the Blacks will take over. He's not a Christian, this is a Christian Nation, what is our country going to end up like?"[15] Another said, "I don't like the fact that he thinks us white people are trash, because we are not."

At a Palin rally in Johnstown, Pennsylvania, amateur camera crews caught crowds yelling out "Osama Obama," "the only difference between Obama and Osama is the BS," "Hussein Mohammed Obama" and "Al Qaeda for Obama"—the confluence of Muslim rumors and terrorist fears—while one heavyset guy sported a Curious George monkey doll with a Obama bumper sticker on its head and paraded it before the camera with a cackle, saying: "This is little Hussein. Little Hussein wanted to see truth and good Americans."[16]

Another incident was revealing in the response it provoked. Two weeks before the election, McCain volunteer Ashley Todd claimed that she had been attacked at an ATM near Pittsburgh by a six-foot-tall, 200-pound black man who saw her McCain bumper sticker, stole $60 and carved a "B" in her face. She said he told her: "You are going to be a Barack supporter."

Todd quickly became a conservative cause célèbre—evidence of an incipient race war that would be no doubt great for ratings and possibly for election results. Fox News senior vice president for news editorial John Moody fired off a grave op-ed on the online FoxForum, titled—ironically, "Moment of Truth."

> It had to happen. Less than two weeks before we vote for a new president, a white woman says a black man attacked her, then scarred her face, and says there was a political motive for it. . . . This incident could become a watershed event in the 11 days before the election. If Ms. Todd's allegations are proven accurate, some voters may revisit their support for Senator Obama, not because they are racists (with due respect to Rep. John Murtha), but because they suddenly feel they do not know enough about the Democratic nominee.[17]

Eighteen hours later, Todd admitted she'd fabricated her tale to get attention for herself and the McCain campaign. A cadre of conservative commentators quietly muttered a collective "never mind," but the impulse to climb the barricades of racial conflict was chilling.

On Election Day, the results of these appeals to "real America" came into clearer focus. In a country that is becoming more diverse and urban, McCain and Palin found their strongest support from older white traditionalist voters in towns with populations under 50,000.[18]

Dig a little deeper and a fuller picture emerges. Yes, Obama did better than past Democratic tickets in many areas—for example, winning Indiana and Virginia for the first time since 1964. But in the Deep South, he did far worse than past Democrats, losing the forty-nine counties of Alabama, Arkansas, Georgia, Mississippi and Louisiana where whites make up 90 percent or more of the population.[19] This is an expression of white minority politics, feeling under siege.

Since the election, the racial gap has only grown. An October *National Journal* poll found job approval for President Obama deeply divided between 43 percent for whites and 74 percent for non-whites while two-thirds of whites believed that living standards for "people like me" wouldn't grow as fast as they had for previous generations. "Whites are not only more anxious," wrote *National Journal*'s Ron Brownstein, "but also more alienated."[20]

The most striking gap is the attitudes between whites and non-whites when it comes to the federal government—

whites don't trust it, non-whites do. It's an old wound that's getting wider.

From the 1860s through the 1960s—from the Civil War to the civil rights era—the federal government was seen as the defender of minorities and an imposition on the white South. During Reconstruction, the federal Freedmen's Bureau was attacked as "an agency to keep the negro in idleness at the expense of the white man," echoing today's "big government" welfare state critiques.[21] The move to disenfranchise African-American voting rights through Jim Crow laws occurred under the cloak of states' rights and a white "counter-revolution" to re-establish local control with the rallying cry "the niggers shall not rule over us!"[22] Almost a century later, when segregation was confronted by Supreme Court rulings, no less than the *National Review* editorialized, "The central question that emerges . . . is whether the White community in the South is entitled to take such measures as are necessary to prevail, politically and culturally, in areas in which it does not predominate numerically. The sobering answering is yes—the White community is so entitled because, for the time being it is the advanced race."[23] White minority politics likes to get dressed up as civic conscience in the face of unconstitutional federal interference: Witness how the White Citizens Councils of the segregated South of the 1950s and 1960s were reborn in the 1980s and 1990s as the Councils of Conservative Citizens.

These fights have deep roots even as they have taken

on new urgency with the presence of an African-American president. One big question remains: How did the Party of Lincoln get left behind on civil rights?

The Party of Lincoln in Name Only

It's an historic irony that the political party that long defended slavery and racial segregation became the first to nominate an African-American for president, while the Party of Lincoln, which fought for Union and advanced civil rights from Reconstruction to Little Rock, has been left with a pathetic lack of diversity on its political bench.

This role reversal is reflected in the GOP's political philosophy as well. Lincoln's Republican Party was the centrist progressive party of its day, expanding individual freedom and embracing change to preserve the union. The modern Republican Party, however, finds philosophical structure in federalism and states' rights, conservative concepts that defined southern Democrats of the John C. Calhoun variety. And perhaps not coincidentally, the party's strongest support now comes from the rebellious states of the former Confederacy.

The legacy of Lincoln and the Civil War has formed the basic fault lines of American politics for the past 150 years, for better and worse. From 1860 to 1960, the current "red" and "blue" states were reversed, with the former slave-owning South voting solidly Democratic for 100 years while Republicans generally dominated the

North. For all the shifts in party labels since then, Southern conservatives have been consistent. They were conservatives because they believed the rights of individual states had primacy over the interfering federal government. Before the Civil War, they did not want their profitable industry restricted or regulated. They wanted to preserve what they saw as a biblically sanctioned way of life. In 1860, the election of Illinois's Abraham Lincoln was enough to make South Carolina fire on Fort Sumter and secede—resisting the results of the election as an unconstitutional usurpation of power. The South did not want northern values imposed upon it. John Wilkes Booth spoke for many in the vanquished South when he shouted *"Sic semper tyrannis"*—"Thus always with tyrants"—after shooting Lincoln at Ford's Theatre days after the end of the war.

During Reconstruction, African-Americans were not only freed but elevated to elected office—including the Congress and governorships—as Republicans. The Knights of the Ku Klux Klan was formed by Confederate veterans like Nathan Bedford Forrest to resist Reconstruction and to intimidate blacks. This was done in the name of defending the integrity of the white southern family, but the larger political agenda was clear: "In effect, the Klan was a military force serving the interests of the Democratic party," wrote historian Eric Foner in his book *Reconstruction*.[24] In time, the federal troops withdrew from the South. Segregation was imposed along with the renewed dominance of the Democratic

Party. The few local Republicans left were brave liberal reformers, a minority party in every sense.

Outside the South—throughout the North, Midwest and West—the smart money remained with the Republicans. From Ulysses S. Grant to William McKinley and Theodore Roosevelt, they were the party of federal power and patronage, the party of industrial expansion and the Gilded Age. All the while, the South stayed stubbornly Democratic. People who lose wars have long memories, and they were not about to vote for the Party of Lincoln.

The pendulum of political power eventually swung back to the Democrats, whose national political dominance reached its peak with FDR's four-term New Deal coalition of liberal reformers, big-city bosses, union leaders, farmers and southern conservatives—held together by the benefits of power and the glue of crises. This coalition began to crack with Harry Truman, who desegregated the armed forces by executive order after World War II as southerners howled. When at the 1948 Democratic convention, the young liberal mayor of Minneapolis, Hubert Humphrey, proposed that the party platform back anti-segregation civil rights legislation, South Carolina Governor Strom Thurmond stormed off the convention floor, leading a delegation of social conservative pro-segregation southern Dixiecrats. He mounted a third-party Dixiecrat campaign for the presidency that year, with the intention of proving the South's power by denying Democrats the White House. Strom won four states in the Deep South—South Carolina, Mississippi,

Alabama and Louisiana, but Truman stayed in the White House.[25]

But it was the expansion of federal power from the Supreme Court of Chief Justice Earl Warren—a Republican former governor of California, appointed to the bench by Eisenhower—that really alienated conservatives and put the Republican Party on the path to renouncing the legacy of Lincoln.

In 1954's *Brown v. Board of Education,* Warren cultivated a unanimous decision outlawing segregation. But some conservatives wanted to stand athwart its history and yell "Stop."

"We consider the Supreme Court's decision in the key segregation cases *(Brown v. Board of Education* and *Bolling v. Sharpe)* to be one of the most brazen acts of judicial usurpation in our history," editorialized the *National Review,* "patently counter to the intent of the Constitution, shoddy and illegal in analysis, and invalid in sociology"[26] The fear of betrayal by the court has persisted in the intensity with which conservatives fight to keep "liberals" off the bench today and renounce alleged RINO (Republican in Name Only) judges like Sandra Day O'Connor.

The ground was shifting beneath the political map. It finally flipped 100 years after the Civil War when southern Democratic President Lyndon Johnson proposed civil rights legislation.

Some conservative Republicans smelled electoral opportunity in the Democrats' shift. It came in the form of

the missing piece of the post–Civil War political puzzle—
the western libertarian conservative. While North and
South were fighting, the West was still being won by pioneers with lots of guns and little government.

Enter Barry Goldwater, born in the Arizona territory
in 1909. Goldwater's libertarian values were clear and
consistent. He helped create the modern conservative
movement with his absolute belief in individual freedom from government control. But there was one gnaw-
ing exception.

Goldwater opposed the Civil Rights Act of 1964. Like
Republican icons Ronald Reagan and George H. W.
Bush, who also opposed the act, Goldwater was no
segregationist—he had desegregated his family's department store and the Arizona Air National Guard. But
on advice from Phoenix lawyer and future Supreme
Court chief justice William Rehnquist, Goldwater decided that the Civil Rights Act was an unconstitutional
infringement upon states' rights.

"It may be just or wise or expedient for Negro children to attend the same school as white children," Goldwater reasoned, "but they do not have a civil right to do
so which is protected by the federal Constitution or
which is enforceable by the federal government."[27]

At the 1964 GOP convention, Goldwater famously declared "Extremism in the defense of liberty is no vice.
And moderation in the pursuit of justice is no virtue."
Jackie Robinson had been campaigning for Goldwater's
primary Republican opponent, New York Governor

Nelson Rockefeller—who was shouted down at the convention for proposing a platform condemning extremist groups such as the Ku Klux Klan. "A new breed of Republicans had taken over the GOP," wrote Robinson. "I had a better understanding of how it must have felt to be a Jew in Hitler's Germany."[28]

On Election Day, Goldwater won only six states—his native Arizona and the deep South, including every state Strom Thurmond carried as a Dixiecrat in 1948. Mississippi cast 87 percent of its votes for Goldwater—the first time the state had voted Republican in its history. In turn, Vermont voted Democratic for the first time in its history.

And so the electoral map began the slide toward the red-blue alignment we know today. When he signed the Civil Rights Act over southern conservative objections, Lyndon Johnson presciently remarked to his press secretary Bill Moyers, "I think we delivered the South to the Republican Party for your lifetime and mine."[29]

Former Senate majority leader Trent Lott was among the many conservative southern Democrats who switched parties in the ensuing decades. In 1984, the Mississippi congressman gave a revealing interview to *Southern Partisan* magazine in which he said, "I think a lot of the fundamental principles that [Confederate President] Jefferson Davis believed in are very important to people across the country, and they apply to the Republican Party."[30] The party labels had changed, but the

southern conservative power structure remained largely
the same. In 2008, a young Republican operative from
Mississippi apologetically told me, "Let's face it—the
base is racist."

The Party of Lincoln may have sold its soul, but the
Faustian bargain contributed to four decades of political
gain. Between 1968 and 2004, Republicans won seven of
ten presidential elections. Before 1968, the opposite was
true—Democrats won seven of ten.

But now the bill is coming due. Demographics are
destiny and America is becoming less white and rural—
more diverse and urban. Republicans find themselves in
danger of becoming a regional party, based in the socially conservative South. In 1999, Republican governors dotted the Northeast in states like New York,
Massachusetts and New Hampshire. Ten years later,
those states are under Democratic control. In New York,
there were thirteen Republican congressmen at the
time—in 2009 there are two. And there is not a single
GOP congressman left in all of New England, the historic home of the Republican Party.

To contemporary ears, it almost sounds like an urban
legend to hear that the first African-American and the
first woman freely elected to the Senate were both Republicans: Edward Brooke of Massachusetts and Margaret Chase Smith of Maine. And here's a stat that puts
the cost of the southern strategy in sharp perspective:
Of the twenty-three African-Americans who served in

Congress before 1900, every single one was a Republican. They would not have dreamed of being anything but members of the Party of Lincoln.

But since the civil rights era, there have been only three African-American Republicans elected to Congress—Senator Brooke and representatives Gary Franks (CT) and J. C. Watts (OK)—while there have been ninety-three Democrats.

The Party of Lincoln has almost entirely lost the allegiance of the African-American community to the point where the reasons for this historical alliance seem dusty and irrelevant. There have been historic appointments of African-American Republicans to high office—such as secretaries of state Colin Powell and Condoleezza Rice—but to date the electoral aspirations of African-American Republicans have been basically DOA because the party is not seen as representing their community.

"They can't appeal to African-Americans and at the same time oppose everything that's in the interest of African-Americans," said former Senator Ed Brooke, now approaching ninety years of age and spending much of the year in the warmth of Miami with his wife, Anne. "When you talk about equality and justice, you can't just preach, you've got to act. That old statement of Abraham Lincoln's—that government should do for people only what they cannot do for themselves—depends on knowing that there are some people who cannot do for themselves. It's got to be a party with a head and a heart."

Brooke told me he applauded the selection of African-American Michael Steele to be the Republican National Chairman, but with a cautionary note: "They made an excellent choice in Michael Steele. . . . But if the desire or hope was that it would generate more African-American or Hispanic votes for the GOP, well it's a good step in the right direction but it's not going to get the job done. . . . I think that alone won't be a change that is sufficient to have masses of African-Americans or all those young people come into the Republican Party."

Young Republicans and Racist E-mails

"*Obama* Bin Lauden [sic] is the new terrorist. . . . Muslim is on there [sic] side . . . need to take this country back from all of these mad coons . . . and illegals."[31]

So typed a man named Eric S. Piker on a Facebook page operated by Audra Shay—a thirty-eight-year-old army veteran, mother and event planner from Louisiana—who was running to be chairman of the Young Republicans.

Shay responded to Piker's post eight minutes later: "You tell em Eric! lol."[32]

It didn't take long for other posters on Shay's page to do the math. First, a regular poster, Derek Moss, wrote: "What's disheartening is the use of the word 'coon' in 2009. Wow . . . I'm usually outnumbered about 500-to-1 on Audra's threads so go ahead, lemme have it, I deserve it." He apparently expected to be criticized among this crowd for calling out the racist comment.

Cassie Wallender, a national committeewoman from the Washington Young Republican Federation, then wrote: "Someone please help a naïve Seattle girl out, is Eric's comment a racial slur?" She answered her own question one minute later: "Okay, why is this okay? I just looked it up. 'It comes from a term baracoons (a cage) where they used to place Africans who were waiting to be sent to America to be slaves.' THIS IS NOT OKAY. And it's not funny."[33]

This was followed soon after by the African-American chairman of the D.C. Young Republicans, Sean L. Conner, who wrote, "I'm really saddened that you would support this type of racial language . . . wow! Thanks Cassie for standing up . . ."[34]

Word started spreading throughout the Young Republican circuit, open to GOP members under forty. For hours, Audra Shay stayed silent.

Finally, she took action. She "de-friended" Wallender and Conner—in the world of Facebook, that means cutting off relations—after calling her out. Piker, who made the original "coon" comment, remained her Facebook "friend."

Shay's immediate concern was damage control. She deleted the controversial exchanges from her page (but not before screenshots were taken) and tried to tamp down the fire internally.

Almost eight hours after Piker's comments, and Shay's ensuing "lol," Shay posted an official-sounding Facebook status update stating that neither she—nor her

Young Republican political slate, ironically called Team Renewal—"condones the use of racial slurs on my wall. . . . It is not right to nor appropriate to talk that way and will not be accepted!" But soon she was back in jaunty country-girl denial mode ("amazed at all the fuss so here is what you need to know. The 6th song on the new Billy Currington CD is the most awesome song!").

At 10:31 p.m., a friend named Dale Lawson raised the P.C. flag, writing "the over reaction to it was a little amusing." Then Eric S. Piker came roaring back: "I agree with dale . . . this is still America . . . freedom of speech and thought is still allowed . . . for now any ways . . . and the last time i checked I was a good ole southern boy . . . and if yur ass is black don't let the sun set on it in a southern town . . ."

The next morning, the black conservative site HipHop Republican.com posted a story on the exchange. "There is a culture war going on inside the Republican Party," one of the site's founders, Lenny McAllister, told me. "At some point, we will see one of two things—either a decline that comes from our inability to move away from the image of an older, exclusive, white-males-only party or to a party that befits the Party of Lincoln, one of more diversity that reflects America today."

It probably doesn't help that Audra Shay grew up dancing in the shadow of a Confederate flag. She was a popular cheerleader for the Southside High School Rebels in Fort Smith, Arkansas, Class of 1990. It was a predominantly white school in those days, with the town's African-American population attending rival Northside High School. The racial disconnect was symbolized by Southside's mascot, Johnny Reb, a Confederate soldier in the mold of Ole Miss's white mustachioed mascot. Supporters would wave the Stars and Bars in the stands. Even then, the mascot came under fire for its politically incorrect imagery. "Save Johnny Reb" was a rallying cry for students who sought to save their mascot from what they saw as censorship.

"I'm ashamed to say it, but looking back, we didn't have many black students, and that kind of stopped many of us from appreciating what the big deal was," explained one former classmate. "In our white suburban neighborhood, cultural conservatism was more important than what political party you belonged to."

After graduating from Southside, Audra attended the University of Arkansas for one year and then joined the army, eventually serving in the Second Infantry Division in Korea. After finishing active duty at Fort Benning, she worked in internal affairs of the Muscogee County Police Department and had the first of two children.

She married for a second time in 1999 and moved to Louisiana, where she opened a small events planning business and got involved in local young Republican politics, eventually serving as field director for pioneering Indian-American Bobby Jindal's first, unsuccessful, gubernatorial campaign. Audra was subsequently hired to be the state grassroots director for the free-market-advocacy organization Americans for Prosperity—which later was instrumental in funding the Tea Parties—and concentrated on climbing the ranks of the national Young Republicans. Her bio proudly states that "she helped to showcase the YRs at the Republican National Committee's Southern Republican Leadership Conference by manning a booth [and] rubbing elbows with Presidential hopefuls."[35]

The Young Republicans have always included a mix of young idealists, aspiring politicos and ideological warriors, and occasionally that combination has veered from ambition into rank ugliness. During the mid-1960s, the crew-cut militants of the young conservative movement had their own scandals to contend with.

One pungent if forgotten incident involved a group of Young Republicans from the mid-Atlantic states known as the "Rat-Finks," who amused themselves with mimeographed racist songbooks at events like the Young Republicans' national conventions. Here is a sample lyric to one choice anti-Semitic number, which was to be sung to the tune of "Jingle Bells":

> Riding through the Reich, in a Mercedes Benz,
> Shooting all the kikes, making lots of friends.
> Rat tat tat tat tat, mow the bastards down,
> Oh what fun it is to have the Nazis back in town![36]

The Rat-Finks were eventually censured in a close vote of twenty-five to nineteen by the Young Republican Federation in 1967, but Audra and others have reason for comfort that scandals don't preclude a life in politics: One of the Rat-Fink's leaders went on to a successful career as a New Jersey state senator and judge.

In the past, racist incidents could be relegated to a distant stack in the library, but now the Internet provides indelible evidence of every racist aside. Racist jokes that may have passed in pool halls and country clubs become permanent proof of callousness and cruelty online.

You'd think the right would have gotten the message when e-mails provided the initial smoking gun in the Jack Abramoff scandals. The story gained traction in part because of the difficult-to-defend sensationalism of e-mails in which Abramoff described his multimillion-dollar Native American casino clients as idiots, troglodytes and monkeys—as in, "I have to meet with the monkeys from the Choctaw tribal council" and "We need to get some money from those monkeys."[37]

They haven't:

- Election Night 2008, South Carolina GOP operative Jeffrey Sewell tweets: "The agony of defeat, we just elected Curious George president." And "Breaking: Obama replaces Secret Service with Black Panthers."[38]

- Florida Republican State Committeewoman Carol Carter sends out the following e-mail a week after the inauguration under the subject line "Amazing!" "How can 2,000,000 blacks get into Washington,

DC in 1 day in sub zero temps when 200,000 couldn't get out of New Orleans in 85 degree temps with four days notice?"[39]

- Los Alamitos, California, Mayor Dean Grose forwarded an e-mail in April showing a watermelon patch lining the White House lawn under the title "No Easter egg hunt this year." He said that he was unaware of racial stereotypes about African-Americans and watermelon. No word, in that case, why he thought the e-mail was funny enough to forward.[40]

- Former South Carolina state election director and Richland County GOP chairman Rusty DePass "joked" on his Facebook page in June that First Lady Michelle Obama was descended from a gorilla which had gone missing from a local zoo: "I'm sure it's just one of Michelle's ancestors—probably harmless."[41] DePass initially reached for a defense from the Scopes Monkey Trial era, claiming that Michelle believed in evolution and was therefore descended from apes. He later apologized to the local NAACP.

- Three days later, Tennessee state legislative aide Sherri Goforth e-mailed out an image labeled "Historical Keepsake"—showing august portraits of all the presidents of the United States, ending with a pair of googly-eyes peering out from a black background to symbolize President Obama.[42] When confronted, the aide to State Senator Diane Black said only that she regretted sending the image to the wrong e-mail list and from her government address. She was "reprimanded" by her supervisors but not otherwise punished (a forced furlough at Memphis's National Civil Rights Museum would have been an inspired penalty).

- Florida neurosurgeon, GOP fundraiser and founder of Doctors for Patient Freedom David McKalip forwarded an image of President Obama as a New Guinea witch doctor with a bone through his nose to a Tea Party listserv group under the subject header "funny stuff." There was a Soviet-style hammer and sickle through the "c" in "Obama Care."[43]

- The million-dollar relaunch of GOP.com hit a snag in October 2009 when its Facebook fan page featured a rogue posting of a photo showing President Obama eating a chicken wing over the old-school racist slogan, "Miscegenation is a crime against American values: Repeal Loving v. Virginia"—the 1967 Supreme Court decision that outlawed bans on interracial marriage.[44]

- When President Obama's speech announcing 30,000 new troops for an Afghanistan surge pre-empted a December '09 airing of a *Charlie Brown Christmas Special,* Arlington, Tennessee, Mayor Russell Wiseman took his frustrations out via Facebook, writing about "our Muslim president." "Try to convince me that wasn't done on purpose. Ask the man if he believes that Jesus Christ is the Son of God and he will give you a 10 minute disertation [sic] about it . . . when the answer should simply be 'yes' . . . you obama people need to move to a muslim country . . . oh wait, that's America . . . pitiful . . . you know, our forefathers had it written in the original Constitution that ONLY property owners could vote, if that has [sic] stayed in there, things would be different."[45]

This is the environment that incubates an incident like the slur on Audra Shay's Facebook page. This time, the uproar grew louder and began to get widespread attention when I wrote about it on The Daily Beast. But Shay was not about to let a little racist e-mail scandal stop her Tracy Flick meets *Strangers with Candy* quest for election.

And so an online whisper campaign against Shay's opponent Rachel Hoff began. An anonymously built temporary Web site targeted Hoff's support for same-sex civil unions as the real scandal, expressed in li'l Lee Atwater tones:

As one of only a very few Young Republicans nationwide in favor of Civil Unions, Rachel Hoff attempted to convince the YRNF in 2007 to adopt a stance IN FAVOR OF CIVIL UNIONS. Although Rachel was not wearing a dress like her female counterparts, but her typical suite [sic], her attempt was met with ridicule and frustration. It was overwhelmingly shot down and left the idea in many delegates minds of: Why would Rachel Hoff support Civil Unions?

Got to love the all-caps for her support IN FAVOR OF CIVIL UNIONS, a brave stance entirely consistent with the party's stated belief in individual freedom (and well short of conservative icon Dick Cheney's belated support for gay marriage). Then there's the weird 1920s-era anti-feminist dig at her for "not wearing a dress like her female counterparts." And the last sentence, with all the subtlety of a Tom DeLay sledgehammer. It's an exceptionally ugly piece of insinuation and propaganda, casting new light on Shay's campaign claim that "the only way to change something you don't like, is to get in and get your hands dirty."

As the two candidates wound their way to the Young Republican Convention in Indianapolis, it became apparent that this was not an isolated incident.

In October 2008, in the wake of news that an effigy of Sarah Palin was being hung outside an affluent Hollywood home as an offensive Halloween decoration, Shay posted: "What no 'Obama in a noose?' Come on now, its [sic] just freedome [sic] of speech, no one in Atlanta would take that wrong! Lol." She picked up the thread again the next morning with a club-footed clarification. "Apparently I could not spell last night. I am wondering if the guys with the Palin noose would care if we had a bunch of homosexuals in a noose."

She posted a conspiracy-theory video that attempted to prove that Obama believes he can only "ensure his own salvation" and "fate" if he helps African-Americans rise above whites, complete with Barnumesque captions ("LISTEN AS HE ATTACKS WHITE PEOPLE").

After Obama's overly cautious take on the Honduran "coup" crisis infuriated Shay, she posted: "This is an outrage and I CAN NOT believe this nation has him as our leader! It makes me sick!" She posted a few minutes later: "My disdain for Obama is directly proportionate for his disdain of this country."

A Facebook friend of Shay's weighed in: "Here's what I am getting tired of: If you call Obama a socialist, terrorist, anti-American, whatever, then you're kinda calling me that, too, cause I voted for him and support him (for the most part). Or, you can claim that I didn't really know what I voted for, and in doing so you're kinda saying I'm ignorant and questioning my intelligence."

Three minutes later, Shay replied: "I think that you are ignorant if you believe this man is anything but anti american. He freely rights [sic] about Marxist philosophies. I never called him a terrorist, but if his policies are socialist (which they are) then what would you call him? His actions speak very loudly and his actions are very anti american. You just can not get past it. You might not like it but the truth is what it is."

With all this ugly information on the table, some thought and hoped that Shay's campaign might collapse under the weight of the Facebook scandal. "I saw something that was morally wrong, and as a conservative I took it upon myself as an individual to stand up, and I do not regret it at all," Cassie Wallender, the Washington State YR national committeewoman, wrote in a letter to the committee. "I was attacked for wanting better for Young Republicans—in my lifetime of work for the Republican Party I have never been accused of being a 'RINO,' until now, by Audra's supporters."

But Kentucky delegate Katherine Miller reflected the myopia of movement politics when she told the *Indianapolis Star*, "This controversy really is not the decisive factor for the majority of people voting here. . . . It really has been played up a little bigger than it really is."[46]

The eventual vote took eight hours, with parliamentary fights to hold a voice vote instead of a secret ballot (it turns out that some conservatives do like card check, if it benefits them). Fistfights nearly broke out between the two camps, and a Hoff supporter from the Oklahoma delegation, who was handing out fliers protesting Shay's Facebook comments, had to be physically removed. "I believe that people were intimidated," said North Carolina delegate John Ross. "Without a secret ballot, many people did not have the opportunity to vote their conscience." In the end, Audra Shay got her prize in a vote of 470 to 415.

"They just took a vote that may have set the party back thirty years," said HipHopRepublican.com's Lenny McAllister, speaking from the floor of the convention hall. "They just voted for a candidate who has a demonstrated tolerance for racial intolerance. She has joked about lynching and then claimed to be a victim. As a black man, I still don't see what's funny about that."

At least Team Renewal had a sense of humor about the oddly named Indianapolis bar where they told supporters to meet after the vote in an irony-free Tweet: "Come join the NEW YRNF Administration at Rock Bottom!!"

POLARIZING FOR PROFIT

We are self-segregating into separate political realities.

Both Fox News and MSNBC have profited from preaching to a narrow but intense audience—conservative Republicans at Fox and liberal Democrats at MSNBC. Loyal viewers see opinion-anchors like Glenn Beck on the right and Keith Olbermann on the left as the only "truth tellers" in town, while dismissing the rest of the media as cowardly or biased. The ideal of objectivity is now dismissed as a myth. We are devolving back to the era when newspapers were owned and operated by political parties.

The attack of the Wingnuts is enabled by an increasingly fragmented and hyper-partisan media. Talk radio and Wingnut Web sites pump up the hate and hyper-partisanship all day, creating a feedback loop of talking points for true believers. They are polarizing for profit. It may be good for ratings, but it's bad for the country.

The result: partisan warfare is on the rise, and trust in media is on the decline. The Pew Research Center for the People & the Press has documented the trend and concluded that "virtually every news organization or program has seen its credibility marks decline" over the past decade.[1]

Even C-Span, which offers unedited coverage of public events without commentary, has experienced a steep—and absurd—decline in believability.[2] In this hyper-partisan environment, people literally don't trust what they see with their own eyes.

The cynicism began with credible accusations of longtime liberal bias inside institutions like CBS News and the *New York Times*. This in turn ignited conservative talk radio and Fox News as alternatives, the latter sold under the slogan "fair and balanced." The idea was sinisterly simple: Only explicit bias could balance the implicit bias of the establishment press.

The problems accelerated with the institution of the "split scream" on twenty-four-hour cable news more than a decade ago—two amped-up partisans from opposing parties screaming talking points at each other, divided by the thin line on your TV screen. The networks pretended that all the heat generated amounted to light as well.

Things have gotten improbably worse with the innovation of the echo chamber—angry people from the same party inciting each other to extremes on television or online, demonizing a phantom opposition and engaging in a partisan pile-on. Half the time it's an amen corner and half a hothouse of hate, a reminder of the old adage that "in a place where everybody thinks alike, nobody thinks very much."

The echo chamber is a route to radicalization. As Cass Sunstein explains in his book *Going to Extremes,* "A good way to create an extremist group, or a cult of any kind, is to separate members from the rest of society. The separation can occur physically or psychologically, by creating a sense of suspicion about non-members. With such separation, the information and views of those outside the group can be discredited, and hence nothing will disturb the process of polarization as group members continue to talk."[3] This dynamic is now occurring on a daily basis.

It's been said that the secret of the demagogue is to make himself as stupid as his audience, so they believe that they are as clever as he. Demagogues are the heroes in the echo chamber. They're selling special knowledge, combining old fears with new technologies and reaching a wider audience than ever before. Their tell-tale signs are much the same as detailed by Richard Hofstadter five decades ago: "The paranoid spokesman sees the fate of this conspiracy in apocalyptic terms. . . . He is always manning the barricade of civilization. He constantly lives at the turning point: It is now or never in organizing resistance to conspiracy. Time is forever just running out."[4]

This apocalyptic urgency is familiar to listeners to talk radio and viewers of opinion-news today. But maybe Wingnut hosts are also nervous because they fear *their* time is running out. What's got them anxious isn't just politics, it's their pocketbook.

Because people have more choices about where to receive their news and opinion, broadcasters are left fighting for a smaller and smaller slice of the pie. "The key to success in modern media is narrow market segmentation," author and columnist David Frum of FrumForum .com explained to me. "It's much better to own *Ski Magazine* than it is to own *Life Magazine*. And it's better to own *Cross Country Ski Magazine* than *Ski Magazine*. The more precise your marketing the more it delivers eyeballs to advertisers. But in politics, you have to put people together, not slice them apart. So the imperative thing for a successful cable network is very different from a successful national political coalition."[5] This dynamic is driving pundits to the political extremes, providing a financial incentive to incite the Wingnuts.

It's a particular problem in talk radio. According to the radio ratings service Arbitron, nearly two-thirds of talk radio's listeners are over age fifty, and almost 90 percent are white: Talk radio is preaching to a declining demographic.[6] It's not surprising that according to some industry experts, talk radio has lost 30 to 40 percent of its ad revenues over the past two years alone.[7] Its slice of revenue is shrinking.

Radio host Michael Medved explained it this way to Tim Mak from NewMajority.com: "In this [economic] environment, you have something of a push to be outrageous, to be on the fringe, because what you're desperately competing for is P-1 listeners [those who tune in most frequently]. And the percentage of people on the fringe who are P-1s is quite high."[8]

As a result, broadcasters who used to present themselves as independent—for example, MSNBC's Ed

Schultz—now dial the partisan anger up to 11 every night. These political performers become prisoners of their own shtick—they cannot evolve or they will be called traitors by the tribe they have cultivated. They can only move in one direction: further out into the extremes.

This dynamic also inspires the peddling of paranoia to pump up ratings. "What Glenn Beck does is spend three shows speculating about whether the Earth is flat," contends Mark Potok of the Southern Poverty Law Center, "and then on the fourth show announces with great fanfare that he, Glenn Beck, has discovered the Earth is round."[9]

Political entertainers pretend to sell ideology and integrity, but what they literally are selling is advertising—and pursuit of coin can also lead to some compromising positions. For example, given the conservatives' criticism of Obama's overspending and invocations of Weimar Republic–like inflation (leading, of course, to the rise of a new Hitler), companies selling gold have been buying up the advertising slots on their shows. Again, Glenn Beck's pitch is typical, blurring the paid advertisement with his personal opinion: "If you've been watching for any length of time, and you still haven't looked into buying gold, what's wrong with you? . . . When the system eventually collapses, and the government comes with guns and confiscates, you know, everything in your home and all your possessions, and then you fight off the raving mad cannibalistic crowds that Ted Turner talked about, don't come crying to me. I told you: get gold."[10]

It's a heated appeal and apparently effective; fear is a powerful motivator. But conflicts of interest were alleged when one advertiser, Peter Epstein of Merit Financial Services, admitted to Politico's Kenneth P. Vogel that gold retailers expect favorable coverage from their commentators. "You pay anybody on any network and they say what you pay them to say," said Epstein. "They're bought and sold."[11]

Loyal audiences are perhaps less understanding of the arrangement. In a complaint filed by Mary Sisak of New Castle, Pennsylvania, she stated that she'd bought gold after she saw a television ad featuring Beck, and online endorsements from radio hosts Fred Thompson and Mark Levin. After spending $5,000, Mary said she learned she could have purchased the same coins for $1,600 less. "How could I be misled by Glenn Beck, Fred Thompson and Marvin [sic] Levin?" she asked. Once you've invested your trust in partisan "truth tellers," heartbreak is sure to follow.

The cycle is self-reinforcing, providing fodder to a larger partisan enterprise. It's a dynamic that David Frum calls the Talk-Fox Complex: "Fox News Broadcasting and the major talk radio shows are staffed by many of the same personalities—like Sean Hannity and Glenn Beck—and they really work together. Talk radio creates a buzz that the news side of Fox then reports on as if it were straight news."[12] One favorite rhetorical bridge is the "some say" formulation, as in "Some say Barack Obama may not be eligible to be president." This is one of the mechanisms by which Wingnuts have been able to hijack our media and, by extension, our politics.

There is a recipe for mainstreaming hyper-partisanship: A rumor is posted on a site like Free Republic and becomes the subject of heated speculation. A site like WorldNetDaily publishes fearmongering as fact or opinion. Now it's got a thin veneer of respectability and a shot at becoming part of the talk radio conversation, often in the form of "just askin'" speculation (as in "Is Obama our first Muslim Marxist president?"). When a Beck or a Rush Limbaugh picks it up, it's hit the big time. It's heading to a protest poster and then a TV screen near you.

The seamless success of this model in creating issues and crafting narratives has made the out-of-power Republican Party effectively subservient to the conservative media crowd. The tail is wagging the dog; partisan media is driving the GOP's message and not the other way around. So Glenn Beck declares, "Our country might not survive Barack Obama," and a few months later, the Republican National Congressional Committee fires off a fundraising letter saying "America cannot survive on this new course."[13] The danger is that the narrow niche-building strategy of partisan news and views is the opposite of the coalition building that political parties use to win elections. Case in point: Glenn Beck.

Beckology

The most influential Wingnut leader in the first year of the Obama administration wasn't an elected official. He isn't even a Republican but an independent conservative—a former Top-40 radio DJ, self-described "borderline schizophrenic"[14] and recovering drug addict turned Mormon convert with a taste for confrontation and confession. He presents a manic mix of politics and religion, loftily billed as "the fusion of entertainment and enlightenment."[15]

In the course of a few years, Glenn Beck has transformed himself from a talk radio curiosity into a multimedia cottage industry, with a nationally syndicated radio show, 5 p.m. Fox News program, a magazine and five books—both fiction and nonfiction—on the bestseller lists.[16] Behind his tearful Mad Hatter act, the man is crazy like a fox—a talented and intelligent radio artist, an entrepreneur of anxiety and redemption. His loyal customers constitute a standing army, and he has already proven they can be deployed at will to the tune of tens of thousands.

"We ♥ Glenn Beck" read a sign at the 9/12 Tea Party rally on the Washington Mall. Each letter was spelled out stadium-style on an individual placard with an American flag filling out the heart. The group holding the placards was clustered under a parchment-colored banner that read "Rainy Day Patriots: We the People Fighting to Restore our Constitutional Republic." Other

evidence of his influence dotted the crowd in the form
of signs and hand-painted T-shirts: "Answer Glenn
Beck's Questions," "God Bless Glenn Beck" and "Glenn
Beck is my Hero."

This was a something of a hometown crowd for Beck.
He had first proposed the rally on air months before,
telling them they were "the only thing standing between slavery and freedom," and more than 50,000 citizens came from across the country.[17] No member of
Congress could have inspired the same attendance.

Over the week of Thanksgiving 2009, Beck came up
with a new cause to coincide with the launch of an up-
coming book—*The Plan*—in August of 2010. With his
ambition hitting new heights, Beck announced the creation of a new political movement, part *Meet John Doe*
and part Father Coughlin, complete with public education seminars. "Today, I have stopped looking for a
leader to show us the way out," Beck declared, "because
I have come to realize that the only one who can truly
save our country . . . is us."[18]

Echoes of Obama's "We are the change we have been
waiting for" aside, self-empowerment is the theme that
runs throughout Beckology. Like a classic evangelical
preacher who connects with his audience by detailing
his days of sin and depravity, Beck uses humor and self-
deprecation to sell his own story of salvation through a
return to personal responsibility. Beck comes armed
with the dry drunk's distrust of the middle ground in
life and politics, where everything is good versus evil,

conservatives versus "the cancer of progressivism," George Washington versus Barack Obama. But in the duel of opposites, nothing compares to the struggle between Good Beck and Bad Beck.

The Good Beck genuinely cares about people and this country. It's one of the things that makes him so emotional on air.

The Bad Beck is such a talented broadcaster that he knows how to manipulate an audience's emotions. He uses fear, anger and resentment to keep their attention day after day, buying his books, attending his rallies.

The two coexist uneasily under the justification that the Bad Beck promotes the Good Beck. He is advancing himself in order to advance a greater cause.

To understand Beck's political appeal, you need a window into his personal life, a story of small-town values remembered from broadcast studios in the skyscrapers of Manhattan. He grew up in Mount Vernon, Washington, a town of 15,000 in those days, perhaps best known as the tulip bulb capital of America. His dad, William, ran a bakery called the Sweet Tooth and the family attended the Immaculate Conception Catholic Church. The town was populated by descendents of Scandinavian immigrants and provided a vision of small-town "real America" that Beck would riff off for decades to come and provide the title for his first book.

But bucolic visions always obscure a more complicated reality. In addition to tulips, Mount Vernon was earning a reputation as the leading marijuana producer in the Pacific Northwest. Nor were things as they seemed on the surface in Beck's family. His mom, Mary, wrestled with addiction and manic depression, leading to a marital split and her death by drowning, which police called an accident but Beck believes was a suicide.

Before she died, Mary gave Glenn a present that would illuminate his life's path: a record collection of classic radio broadcasts called *The Golden Age of Radio*. "I was mesmerized by the magic radio was," Beck remembers, "how it could create pictures in my head."[19] He became a student of the art form, idolizing pioneers like Orson Welles and practicing his radio voice into a tape recorder in his bedroom.

By the time he was a junior in high school, Beck was commuting to Seattle by bus every weekend to broadcast on a local FM rock station. He was also on the road to smoking pot every day for the next fifteen years (by his own estimation) and spinning records by late '70s white-bread rock troika of Cheap Trick, Supertramp and Electric Light Orchestra.

Rock 'n' roll radio would be Glenn Beck's university. By 1983, at the age of nineteen, Beck was the youngest morning radio show host in the nation, broadcasting from the military enclave of Corpus Christi, Texas. He was a one-man Morning Zoo, with on-air skits and imaginary guests like a clueless Muppet-voiced foil Beck named "Clydie Clyde," which still appears in his act.

Beck's mentor and manager at the station was a former marine and surfing Mormon named Jim Sumpter. "I never had a doubt that Glenn was headed for huge things," Sumpter told me on the phone from his radio show studio in Florida, "but I didn't see any indication of an interest in politics. I never for a moment dreamt that Glenn was, based on his lifestyle choices, a political conservative. If you asked me if Glenn would have ever been on the cover of *Time* magazine I would have asked you what you were smoking."

Beck was channeling the decade of excess, doing cocaine, driving a DeLorean and cultivating a collection of thin ties. He played the fool but did not suffer fools. "When we were in Texas, Glenn hated Texans, hated 'em," Sumpter said. "Now he talks about how he just loves the people in Texas. He used to make fun of them—their belt buckles, the chunky jewelry, I mean the whole deal. And he just hated Mormons."

It wasn't just Mormons. Beck's self-described mantra at the time was "I hate people." Despite occasionally sharing the mic with a chimp named Zippy, despair was seeping in and Beck's mood swings were alienating colleagues; one remembered him as "a sadist, the kind of guy who rips the wings off flies." His competitive edge could certainly contain a cruel streak. When he faced off against a former friend in the Phoenix market, Beck called up the man's wife on air after she had a miscarriage and mocked his friend-turned-rival, saying it was evidence that he couldn't do anything right—he couldn't even have a baby.[20]

Beck's own personal life was suffering. His first marriage was crumbling and a daughter was born with cerebral palsy. Amid drug use and manic behavior, Beck wrestled with suicidal fantasies, writing later, "There was a bridge abutment in Louisville, Kentucky, that had my name on it. . . . Every day I prayed for the strength to be able to drive my car at 70 mph into that bridge abutment. I'm only alive today because (a) I'm too cowardly to kill myself . . . and (b) I'm too stupid."[21]

By his late twenties, the one-time radio wunderkind had burned most professional bridges and found himself working at a radio station in New Haven, a comparative Siberia from previous postings. Divorced and with drug use and alcoholism spiraling out of control, Beck hit bottom. He went to his first AA meeting in 1994 and began a skeptic's search for faith, starting with a self-taught great books seminar that included tomes from Hitler, Carl Sagan and Pope John Paul II and culminating with his baptism into the Mormon Church.

Personal rebirth was followed by professional rebirth. Clean, sober and remarried, Beck was tiring of the bubble-gum Top-40 morning-zoo format. Talk radio icons like Rush Limbaugh and WABC's race-baiting Bob Grant were his on-air idols now. Beck began peppering his banter with political references and pushing executives for a talk show to call his own. In January 2000, the Glenn Beck show debuted in Tampa Bay. "I don't really consider myself a conservative. I know I don't consider myself a liberal," he said. "I have a brain and I like to use it sometimes."[22]

In 2006, CNN's Headline News brought him to cable television to host a political talk show from an independent perspective. But Beck chafed against the billing and enjoyed only middling ratings. He was liberated by an offer from Fox News and the election of Barack Obama.

The Glenn Beck Program debuted on Fox News the night before Obama's inauguration, and he came out swinging. Sarah Palin was among the first night's guests. and within weeks Beck was pumping up "the Road to Communism" and offering "Comrade Updates," declaring "the destruction of the West is happening"[23] and that "the president is a Marxist . . . who is setting up a class system."[24]

Sometimes he pivoted his imagery to the right, saying "The government is a heroin pusher using smiley-faced fascism to grow the nanny state"[25] and claiming that "the federal government is slowly drifting into fascism." Other times he indulged both sides of the spectrum, as on April 2, when Beck asked, "Is this where we're headed?" and showed images of Hitler, Lenin and Stalin.[26]

Beck's opposition to the health-care bill in the summer of '09 hit all the bases. First there was fascism, as in the "[health-care] system is going to come out the other side dictatorial—it's going to come out a fascist state."[27] Then there was health care as "good old socialism . . .

raping the pocketbooks of the rich to give to the poor."[28] And finally, race: "The health care bill is reparations. It's the beginning of reparations."[29]

Beck's ratings soared, and his credibility was bolstered by on-air investigations into Obama personnel like "Green Jobs czar" Van Jones, who had in fact once described himself as a communist and signed a 9/11 Truther petition calling for an investigation into whether President Bush had known in advance about the attacks of September 11th. Beck hammered home the story while other news outlets resisted it. Jones ultimately resigned. Beck had both a scoop and a scalp.

Beck's newfound firebrand politics and effectiveness in driving the news cycle had some old friends scratching their heads. "I never got the impression that Glenn is as naturally curious as he appears to be, to be bringing the information forward that he is," said Jim Sumpter. "I don't know if Glenn's being fed or if Glenn's really the driving force. I have no idea. If he's the driving force, that's a Glenn Beck I never saw. If he's being fed, then the showmanship that goes into all of this is classic Beck. Now if Glenn is the showman and the driving force behind bringing the information to the forefront, then, then I think we're probably looking at near genius in terms of what he's doing . . . [but] I don't think this is Glenn. The catalyst in this thing is not Glenn. Glenn's the vehicle, not the catalyst."

Catalyst or not, Beck was hitting all the Wingnut themes with perfect pitch. When Iowa's court legalized gay marriage, Beck declared, "I believe this case is actually about going into churches, and going in and attacking churches and saying, 'You can't teach anything else.'"[30] To nervous gun rights advocates, he asserted that Obama "will slowly but surely take away your gun or take away your ability to shoot a gun, carry a gun."[31] He brought avowed secessionists on his show and gave them an interested hearing. Beck drew the widest denunciations when he called President Obama "a racist" with a "deep-seated hatred for white people."[32] An advertiser boycott began, but the zealotry of his advocates more than compensated as yet another Beck book went up the charts in 2009. First there was *Glenn Beck's Common Sense: The Case Against an Out-of-Control Government* and then *Arguing with Idiots: How to Stop Small Minds and Big Government,* featuring Beck leering on the cover in a Soviet-style commissar's uniform.

In the books, as on air, it's always a wrestling match between the Good Beck—humorous, self-effacing and calling on a higher power for a sense of purpose—and the Bad Beck, peddling political apocalypse, the opinion equivalent of a horror film: "We are a country that is headed towards socialism, totalitarianism, beyond your wildest imagination."[33] "There is a coup going on. There is a stealing of America . . . done through the guise of an election."[34]

Beck's message resonates beyond Main Street and the Tea Party protests. Down in the white supremacy cesspool of Stormfront, some contributors thought they recognized a fellow traveler. "Glen [sic] Beck can be useful," wrote SS_marching. "When Glen beck said 'Obama Has A Deep-Seated Hatred For White People' he is able to reach a much wider audience than we can. They will [be] predisposed to the idea and the next time Obama pushes an anti-white policy they will see it as such."[35]

Frequent Stormfront poster Thor357 sees Beck as a recruiting tool: "I have talked to 6 people in two days because Glenn Beck woke them up, it's amazing how angry they are. They are pissing fire over Obama, this is a good thing. Now I educate them."[36] Carolina Patriot poster takes a down-home view: "Every now and again when an infomercial takes the place of hunting or fishing, I'll turn over to Glenn Beck if he's on and watch his show. Sometimes it is amusing, sometimes it is informed, and sometimes, I think he comes to SF [Stormfront] to steal show ideas."[37]

QHelios gives Beck the benefit of the doubt: "By no means do I think [Beck] is aware of the racial issue, and for the moment that is ok . . . He is stirring the pot, and I thank him for that."[38]

Olbermania

In the beginning there was Phil Donahue. The soft and snowy-haired advocate of liberal causes, a caring, not confrontational '70s-style talk show host—he wanted to feel your pain.

Then there was Keith Olbermann—he wants you to feel his pain.

Liberals' new assertiveness accompanied the rise of this unlikely on-air advocate, a sportscaster turned straight news anchor turned partisan pit bull.

Smart, funny and acerbic, Olbermann also has a reputation for being prickly and paranoid. But his instinct to pick fights provided important utility: At a time when conservative opinion anchors were ruling the cable news world, Keith Olbermann decided to return fire.

Here's a measure of his success. When Olbermann started his eight p.m. show, Countdown, on MSNBC in 2003 there were no overtly liberal prime-time anchors in all of cable news. Now his network is seen as the liberal corollary to Fox, featuring a full line-up of liberals in the orbit of his eight p.m. slot.

Aiming to echo the moral authority of Edward R. Murrow down to his lift of "Good Night and Good Luck," Olbermann trades in self-righteous indignation. His signature schtick is the special commentary, five minutes of Keith staring right into the camera delivering a diatribe that he has written himself. It's a radio sermon made for TV, delivered in a born broadcaster's baritone. His targets are anyone—or anything—to his political right.

It's tempting to describe his commentary style as full-contact, to reach for an available sports metaphor for combat, but it wouldn't be accurate—because Olbermann doesn't have guests on his show who disagree with him. It is an amen corner, an echo chamber presented as a truth-telling moment for America. Keith Olbermann isn't interested in any opinion but his own.

Like his rising alter-ego Glenn Beck, Olbermann had his roots in radio, a precocious if isolated teenager running a half-watt station at his high school in Westchester, New York, and then graduating to the Cornell University radio station. His love of radio is evident in his pauses and diction, delivering a point with dramatic effect. He doesn't talk so much as deliver.

But it wasn't politics but sports that drove him, and after bouncing around local sportscaster gigs in regional markets, he landed at ESPN in 1992, selected to co-host *SportsCenter* at eleven p.m. with Dan Patrick. Their repartee redefined the model, with amped-up humor and sly asides ("If you're scoring at home, or even if you're alone . . .") they mocked the formalities of the format and made the show an event, a return to the frat house for exhausted adults. Most of all, they made the news fun to watch, a lesson that would last.

But Olbermann did not last at ESPN. In 1997, at the height of his public popularity as a sportscaster he left. One colleague recalled, "He didn't burn bridges, he napalmed them."[39]

Olbermann's reputation as a malcontent would dog him as he hosted shows on Fox and MSNBC. Sometimes contracts were not renewed, sometimes he was fired. After an ESPN exposé portrayed Keith as a sour, insular man who made co-host Suzy Kolber cry after shows, Olbermann felt compelled to write a public mea culpa in Salon.com. More than a face-saving PR stunt, the 2002 essay was a reflective walk through Olbermann's psyche, full of competing insecurities and perfectionism: "I have lived much of my life assuming much of the responsibility around me and developing a dread of being blamed for things going wrong," he wrote. "If anything would have cut through my neuroses, it would've been a colleague's tears. If I had known, I think I could've jumped over the fence I'd built around myself and said what the inner guy always knew: No TV show is worth crying over. Suzy: I'm sorry."[40]

In 2003, Olbermann got a rare second chance to host a prime-time show on a network he'd left on strained terms, MSNBC. *Countdown* was a late March replacement for Phil Donahue's brief return to television, a ratings failure that was seen as the end of experimenting with liberal views in prime time. "MSNBC takes sharp right turn," was one typical reading of the tea leaves. Ironically, the night of Olbermann's debut, he announced, "Our charge for the immediate future is to stay out of the way of the news. . . . News is news. We will not be screwing around with it."

He played it straight down the middle and enjoyed middling ratings. He cultivated a feud with Fox News's Bill O'Reilly, naming him one of "the worst persons in the world" more than fifty times in four years.[41] He re-enacted news stories with puppets (another thing he shares with Glenn Beck). Humor was his calling card as a news broadcaster. His personal political beliefs were unknown even to people close to him, and Olbermann has said he doesn't vote.[42]

But that profile changed dramatically in August 2006. Then–general manager Dan Abrams had written a memo encouraging hosts to offer opinions on air. Waiting for a flight at LAX, Olbermann happened upon a speech given by Bush Secretary of Defense Donald Rumsfeld in which he compared opponents of the administration's war and counter-terror strategy to Nazi appeasers, saying that America was fighting "a new type of fascism." Fired up and fueled by a few screwdrivers, Olbermann wrote his first special comment.

"The man who sees absolutes where all other men see nuances and shades of meaning is either a prophet or a quack," he began. "Donald H. Rumsfeld is not a prophet." Olbermann accused the secretary of impugning "the morality or intelligence—indeed, the loyalty—of the majority of Americans who oppose the transient occupants of the highest offices in the land. . . . This is a Democracy. Still. Sometimes just barely. And as such, all voices count—not just his."[43]

It was a forceful but odd addition to prime time, a counter-speech with an inner history nerd erupting from within: Churchill, Neville Chamberlain, Hitler, Nixon, Joe McCarthy, General Curtis LeMay and Ed Murrow all mentioned within five minutes. The audiences loved it. The special commentaries continued and ratings spiked along with the rhetoric.

Olbermann offered thirteen more special commentaries in 2006, dialing up the outrage, casting himself as the liberal avenger against the Bush administration. "Bush: Pathological Liar or Idiot-in-Chief?" he asked. He accused Bush of "panoramic and murderous deceit," having an "addled brain" and "laying waste to Iraq to achieve your political objectives" and told the president to "Shut the hell up!"—all in one broadcast. He argued that "the leading terrorist group in this country right now is the Republican Party,"[44] called on Bush to resign, hinted at impeachable offenses and—in an apocalyptic riff worthy of Glenn Beck—said his policies could bring about "the beginning of the end of America."[45] All this led *New York* magazine to pay him the ultimate bittersweet compliment, calling Olbermann "the Limbaugh of Lefties."

When Secretary of State Condoleezza Rice compared Saddam Hussein to Hitler, Olbermann's wrath was again predictably vast. "Invoking the German dictator who subjugated Europe; who tried to exterminate the Jews; who sought to overtake the world is not just in the poorest of taste, but in its hyperbole, it insults not merely the victims of the Third Reich, but those in this country who fought it and defeated it."[46]

True. But Olbermann himself couldn't help but wade into the hyperbole and equivalency game at times, calling Bush a "fascist" and acting "dictatorial." One of his favorite routines was offering a Nazi *Sieg Heil* salute while holding a picture of Bill O'Reilly across his face, prompting the Anti-Defamation League to write a strained letter of complaint. "Your repeated use of the Nazi salute has resulted in many complaints from our constituents, including Holocaust survivors and their families. . . . In light of these concerns, we hope that you will reconsider your use of the Nazi salute in the future."[47]

The subject of rival Fox News drove Olbermann even deeper into a frenzy of moral equivalency. "Al-Qaeda really hurt us but not as much as Rupert Murdoch has hurt us, particularly in the case of Fox News. Fox News is worse than al-Qaeda—worse for our society. It's as dangerous an organization as the Ku Klux Klan ever was. Fox News will say anything about anybody and accepts no criticism. Half the people there ought to be in an insane asylum."[48] Pot, meet kettle.

With Bush out of office, some wondered how Olbermann would fare without nightly opposition. They shouldn't have worried. After Obama backed an extension of the Bush administration policy on warrantless wiretapping, Olbermann declared: "Welcome to change you cannot believe in."[49] As a series of pragmatic compromises on health care began to enrage the party's left wing, the Olbermann of the Bush years came boiling back to the surface. With the public option effectively out of the picture, Olbermann started making demands of the president. "It is, above all else, immoral and a betrayal of the people who elected you, Sir. You must now announce that you will veto any bill lacking an option or buy-in, but containing a mandate."[50] He named centrist Democrat Senator Ben Nelson "the worst person in the world" for comparing him to Limbaugh and Beck, while suggesting that Independent-Democrat Senator Joe Lieberman drive off a bridge.[51] And he went after conservative commentator Michelle Malkin by saying that without her "total mindless, morally bankrupt, knee-jerk, fascistic hatred" she "would just be a big mashed up bag of meat with lipstick on it."[52]

The certainty and moral outrage have not yet faded. It reminds me of something a wise man once said: "The man who sees absolutes where all other men see nuances and shades of meaning is either a prophet or a quack."

Wingnuts on the Web

Harry Truman used to say that "the only thing new in the world is the history you don't know." Harry Truman never met the Internet.

The Internet is a force multiplier for Wingnuts, empowering them to reach far broader audiences faster than ever before. It is the best breeding ground for every imaginable conspiracy theory. It provides a national megaphone for what would in earlier years have been just a whisper campaign. It enables like-minded individuals to ignore geography and their isolation and come together as an opinion army.

While the right was dominating talk radio, the left rallied its partisans through the Internet. Within a few years groups like MoveOn.org and blogs like Daily Kos went from being outside agitators to inside players.

Their fund-raising powers and ability to fire up activists were too impressive for the Democratic establishment not to forgive and forget their outbursts of radicalism: MoveOn's infamous "General Petraeus or General Betray Us?"[53] and the comments of Daily Kos founder Markos Moulitsas after the killing of four military contractors in Iraq. ("I feel nothing over the death of mercenaries. . . . They are there to wage war for profit. Screw them."[54])

The GOP was slower to adapt from the AM dial. There were popular and influential conservative news aggregators like the Drudge Report that filtered the news though a subjective lens but very little in terms of effective on-line activist organizing. During the 2008 campaign, I'd been told by a conservative strategist that "our voters don't use the Internet"—while he was surfing the Web. The McCain-Palin campaign seemed to take that advice to heart (no doubt under the influence of the direct-mail mandarins who'd made their fortunes while building the conservative movement). Republicans even sent out a fund-raising letter designed to look like an emergency telegram—the instant message of the horse-and-buggy era—two years after the last real telegram was sent by Western Union. They were the Party of the Telegraph.

The technology gap could be seen in the GOP's 2008 online outreach. Obama had 3.1 million Facebook supporters, compared to 600,000 for McCain. Obama had 113 million YouTube views compared to twenty-five million for McCain. And when it came to Meetup.com— a site famously used by Howard Dean supporters in

2004—McCain got outhustled not only by Obama but also Libertarian candidate Bob Barr. McCain ran a twentieth-century GOTV (Get Out the Vote) campaign in which phone calls and mailings to supporters were the key metric. The McCain campaign spent $18 million in postage and shipping costs, and $3 million on the Internet, according to opensecrets.org. By comparison, Obama spent $15 million in postage and shipping costs and $14 million on the Internet.

But after the election, grassroots conservatives woke up to social media and the Internet. They were energized by being in the opposition—supplementing their talk radio diet with Twitter, the social networking service that pushes text messages of 140 characters or less. Ironically, McCain—whose campaign hadn't collected cell phone numbers for text messaging during the campaign—created his own Twitter account three days after the election and ten months later had a million followers.[55] By mid-2009 there were twice as many conservative congressmen on Twitter as Democrats, and Sarah Palin was using her Facebook page as her primary means of communicating with supporters. The Tea Parties and town hall protests were organized online, and with an assist from Fox News' pre-game promotion, they started to feel like populist uprisings.

This conservative netroots revolution is an evolutionary leap—a higher degree of specialization—beyond the niche partisan network approach innovated by Roger Ailes at Fox News. Now what conservatives dismiss as

"mainstream media"—because it does not reflect movement politics—can be completely bypassed. You can
have news tailored to fit your beliefs and chat with like-
minded activists. The logical conclusion is already upon
us: conservatives trying to create their own online ency-
clopedia, an alternative to Wikipedia known as Conser-
vapedia.[56] It's the actual expression of what Stephen
Colbert only joked about when he denounced reference
books as "elitist—constantly telling us what is or isn't
true or what did or didn't happen."[57]

   In the isolation of the echo chamber, the influence of
fringe news sites is increased, and the tallest midget in
that corner of the Wingnut world is WorldNetDaily. It
was the brainchild of Joseph Farah, a mustachioed longtime newspaperman from Paterson, New Jersey, turned
outer-limits conservative activist. Farah was a generation
older than most Internet entrepreneurs, but as editor of
the *Sacramento Union* in California he'd gotten to know
the Silicon Valley crowd and saw the news potential of
the evolving medium. Farah convinced his friend Rush
Limbaugh to pen front-page columns for the *Sacramento
Union*. It was too late for the *Union;* circulation continued
to decline and the paper soon shut its doors, but subsequently Farah embarked on a career as a Clinton critic
from the perch of the Western Journalism Center, funded
by Richard Mellon Scaife (and including the then-con-
servative Arianna Huffington on its board of advisors).

   At the time, right-wing opposition to Bill Clinton was
still essentially an analog event, pumped out over radio,

magazines, direct mail and videotapes that purported to offer evidence of rape, murder and drug deals perpetrated by the forty-second president. While repeatedly "investigating" a conspiracy theory that longtime Clinton aide Vince Foster had not committed suicide but had been murdered with the White House's knowledge—a theory determined to be false by three official reports—Farah began aggregating anti-Clinton articles on a site called eTruth.com. He upped the ante in 1997 with the launch of WorldNetDaily with his wife and quickly claimed to have 10,000 visitors a day.

Twelve years and two presidents later, WorldNetDaily has established itself as a clearing house of right Wingnut information and paraphernalia with twenty-five employees. Visitors have spiked since Obama's election.[58] Farah claims an impressive six to eight million unique visitors a month, and $400 million in annual sales from its superstore, peddling books like *Muslim Mafia* and $80 jars of earth from Jerusalem's Temple Mount while offering special departments for Tea Party paraphernalia. There are gimmicks to trade on voter anger, like a "pink slip" you can send to every member of Congress for the discounted price of $29.95, and a lawn sign with the motto "America was founded by Right-Wing Extremists."

The gear may be profitable but it's the stories that keep people coming. With its blurring of news and opinion, WorldNetDaily draws a devoted audience, claiming credit for breaking the Obama–Bill Ayers connection,[59]

Hamas's alleged endorsement of Obama[60] and investigations into Obama's Chicago church.[61] Some of its stories are picked up by other conservative outlets quietly and not a little shamefacedly because of the sub-tabloid reputation of the outfit. ("Glenn Beck was reading WorldNet-Daily copy without attribution and that's how he ended up claiming the scalp of Van Jones," Farah told me.)

But aspirations to credibility are diminished with stories about H1N1 microchip implants[62] and FEMA concentration camps,[63] leading to nicknames like WorldNut Daily. And for all the biblical beliefs professed on the site (such as creationist-inspired stories that try to debunk ideas that fossil fuels came from fossils) and strict stands against pornography, there is preoccupation with proving Democratic opponents are secretly gay. The site repeatedly published a thoroughly discredited drifter's claim that "he took cocaine in 1999 with the then-Illinois legislator [Obama] and participated in homosexual acts" with him[64] and regurgitated bilge about Hillary Clinton's "well-known bisexuality and her lesbian affair with her beautiful assistant."[65] All in all, it offers a relentlessly grim prognosis for America short of the second coming (predicted in 2015),[66] full of plans for Obama to bring back "inquisitions"[67] and "destroy capitalism."[68] No wonder its primary advertiser appears to be "survival seeds" for your very own "crisis garden" and a "crisis cooker" to "prepare hot meals when the power is off."[69] They are profiting off the paranoia they intentionally inflame in their readers.

But the real growth industry for WorldNetDaily in
2009 was their enthusiastic advocacy of Birther claims
that Obama was not born in the United States and is
therefore ineligible to be president. Farah rented twenty
roadside billboards saying "Where's the Birth Certificate?" at a cost of $300,000 and collected online dona-
tions to help fund the effort. A WND-produced DVD "A
Question of Eligibility" documents the claims of Birther
proponents including Alan Keyes and Orly Taitz, but
darkly states that credits for the movie are being with-
held by the filmmakers because "they fear reprisals
from their government."

Farah sees himself as an old-school newspaper editor
rather than a partisan advocate. He claims to take a dis-
interested view of the op-eds on his homepage. "You
ought to see some of the wacky stuff that they write.
Doesn't mean I agree with it," he told me. "I don't even
look at the columns before they get published in World-
NetDaily. We have a commentary editor who does
that. . . . I don't even read most of the commentary in
WorldNetDaily *after* it's published ' cause I'm not a
commentary kind of a guy, to be honest with you."

His own commentaries, however, are a different matter, and they do not pretend to be the work of a journalist aiming for objectivity. Instead, the political and the
religious are often entwined with a relentlessly hostile
view of Democrats in general and President Obama in
particular. On Inauguration Day, for example, Farah
offered readers a specially written prayer for the

president's failure: "I do not hesitate today in calling on godly Americans to pray that Barack Hussein Obama fail in his efforts to change our country from one anchored on self-governance and constitutional republicanism to one based on the raw and unlimited power of the central state. It would be folly to pray for his success in such an evil campaign. I want Obama to fail because his agenda is 100 percent at odds with God's. Pretending it is not simply makes a mockery of God's straightforward Commandments."[70]

At the end of Obama's first year, did Farah agree with the calls to impeach Obama that are advertised on his site? "Oh, hell yeah, I think there are grounds for impeaching Obama. I think there were grounds for impeaching Bush. I think there were grounds for impeaching Clinton . . . There's nothing in the Constitution that would even remotely justify a national takeover of health care. [Before the election] I predicted that Americans would wake up from this slumber that they've been [in] for so long and start marching in the streets again to reclaim their liberties and that's exactly what I see happening today. Obama could end up being, [in the] long term, a blessing in disguise."

I ask whether he worries whether WND's stories could provoke an ugly response from an unstable reader. "I think the media establishment should ask themselves that question. When they see hundreds of thousands of Americans rallying in Washington and call it tens of thousands and ignore grassroots protest movements around the country, they are doing a disservice to a vibrant debate in a free republic. They are promoting other methods for grievances to be addressed. There are only a few other possibilities—peaceful civil disobedience is one, and violent force is another. I believe reporting events accurately is the best protection of a vibrant debate in a free republic. Covering up events and silencing voices is much more irresponsible and dangerous."

Farah doesn't deny that WND's stories add to the heat on the Wingnut street, but says, "I don't think anger is necessarily an all bad thing. We should be angry at Hitler. We should be angry at Charles Manson." But what about when people start comparing President Obama to Hitler? I ask. "Well, if the analogy fits, it would be irresponsible not to make it," he replies. "Obviously, you can't compare him to Hitler's genocidal holocaust policies, right? He hasn't done anything remotely resembling that. But I think it's fair to point out that Hitler nationalized health care and that Stalin did that and Hugo Chávez did that and Fidel Castro did that."

For WorldNetDaily and others on the Wingnut Web, extremism in defense of liberty is no vice.

Escaping the Echo Chamber

The pioneering television journalist Edward R. Murrow said, "To be persuasive, we must be believable; to be believable we must be credible; to be credible we must be truthful."[71]

Truth, or course, doesn't come tailor-made for any one ideology or political party.

But hyper-partisanship has become an industry unto itself, and it is thriving at a time when the old news industry, aspiring to objectivity dominated by print reporting and the network evening news, seems to be fading. The fragmentation and self-segregation we are experiencing with television, radio and the Internet exacerbates our political differences while they decrease the confidence we had in the honesty and integrity of journalism altogether.

Today, with newspapers fighting for survival, faith in the accuracy and fairness of the press is at twenty-five-year lows.[72] You can't blame people for being cynical. The clearest path to profit seems to come from abandoning the ideal of objectivity and nakedly playing to the base. But even at a time when pundits sound like paid shills for political parties, it was shocking to learn that black conservative columnist Armstrong Williams had accepted a quarter of a million taxpayer dollars from the Bush administration to promote its No Child Left Behind education policy in print and on air.[73]

Ironically, Williams had previously complained about the partisan straightjacket he felt imposed upon him by the split-scream formatting of cable news, telling Tina Brown on CNBC, "One of the things that I struggle with when I go on television like, let's say, a *Crossfire,* [or] Wolf Blitzer, I'm expected to take a certain side. I'm expected to defend the president [Bush]. Now there are

some areas I don't want to defend the president in because I don't necessarily believe that, but you're put in
that position. And I think sometimes you're in a
predicament that the public is not really getting what
you think is their best interests served. So I think sometimes we get caught up in these labels and these stereotypes . . . [and] we do the public a disservice."[74]

The spin cycle is baked into the booking of guests
where predictable partisanship is encouraged. Conflict
sells and balanced analysis is considered bad for ratings—it takes too long to get to the truth.

Politicians have an interest in encouraging an increasingly partisan media. By drumming home the message of
media bias, they try to diminish the credibility of their
critics while developing contacts more likely to present
their side of the story. This self-serving mission requires
loss of perspective. Texas Republican Congressman
Lamar Smith, for instance, told students in the summer
of '09 what he believed to be the "the greatest threat to
America." It was not necessarily a recession, he said, or
even another terrorist attack. "The greatest threat to
America is a liberal media bias."[75]

Washington is the only city in the nation where the
most important thing about you is what political party
you belong to. Partisan media reinforces the rampant
"team-ism." If you walk into a congressman's office and
see Fox News on the TV and a *Washington Times* on the
table, you'll immediately know what party he or she be-
longs to, just as you would if MSNBC was blaring or the

Washington Post was the paper of choice. It's no surprise that Republicans and Democrats are so divided.
They are consuming different versions of the truth, in-
terpreting the same events in fundamentally different
ways.

Likewise, the echo chamber isolates and intensifies
grassroots politics, breeding groupthink in tiny platoons
that can have disproportionate influence on political debates. When it extends to a national level, it can create a
Tower of Babel, condemning us to mutual incomprehen-
sibility. It's easier to demonize people who disagree with
you if you don't know them. In the constant partisan
spin cycle everyone has lost sight of the fact that only 15
percent of Americans call themselves conservative Republicans and only 11 percent describe themselves as
liberal Democrats.[76] Slicing and dicing that demographic is going to produce diminishing returns, while
leaving the other 74 percent of Americans in the center
available and unaccounted for.

There are already signs of a demand for something
different. In 2009, a *Time* magazine online poll found
that the *Daily Show*'s Jon Stewart was the most trusted
man in news.[77] When self-professed "fake news" sur-
passes real news in terms of credibility, it can be
counted as a serious protest vote against the status quo.
Media manipulation by professional partisans on both
sides has become so predictable that satire has emerged
as the last best way to cut through the spin cycle. Viewers' intelligence is respected even as they are enter-

tained, and between laughs the civic backbone begins to straighten a bit because someone is calling "bullshit." If humor can help rebalance politics by pointing out the absurdities of what passes for debate, it is preferable to the split scream or the echo chamber. It's even better if the proponent punches both left and right as a matter of principle. More examples of independence might be what it takes for the news industry to be trusted again as the honest brokers of American politics.

SARAH PALIN AND
THE LIMBAUGH BRIGADES

The morning after the 2008 election, David Kelly hung the American flag upside down outside his Colorado Springs home.

"I felt our nation was in distress, going in the wrong direction," he explained. "I was exercising my God-given, unalienable right as a citizen of this great nation to express myself. That flag in distress was telling me and my whole neighborhood that our nation is in distress and we must stand tall and turn the tide."

A week later, Kelly filed papers to form the Draft Sarah 2012 Committee.

"Sarah Palin represents the silent majority of this nation, which I think scares the left and the liberal media," the self-described Scotch-Irish American told me. "She's everybody's mom or sister or the girl next door. They can imagine themselves running into her at the supermarket and having casual conversation . . . She just invokes and embodies what conservative America's all about: God and County."

Rarely has anyone gone from obscurity to obsession in America's psyche faster than Sarah Palin.

Her supporters feel a personal connection to the

woman they see as a salt-of-the-earth supermom, a straight talking, pro-life, pro-gun icon—the face of conservative populism. Her detractors call her the Queen of the Wingnuts.

Geraldine Ferraro, she ain't. She's been able to parlay a historic but losing vice presidential bid into the kind of devotion that leads supporters to sleep in parking lots to meet her, buy a million copies of her memoir in less than a month and push her into the front runner's circle for the 2012 GOP presidential nomination.

Not bad for someone who was a small-town Alaskan mayor at the start of the decade and spent just thirty-two months governing America's forty-ninth most populous state before quitting. But there's a slight wrinkle in this conservative Cinderella story: Sixty-three percent of Americans have said they would "never" consider voting for her for president.[1]

This stark enthusiasm gap reflects the deep disconnect between conservative populist true believers and the rest of the country. It is reinforced by the Wingnut media and their followers, who overflow small venues, turning them into amen corners. In this environment, there are no enemies on the right and no such thing as too extreme—the more outrageous a statement, the more it will be applauded. Narrow but intense support may be good for ratings. It may even be enough to take over a political party. But if it is defiantly uninterested in reaching out, can it lead it to national victory?

When John McCain announced her as the surprise

pick for VP in late August of '08 Sarah Palin's profile was very different. Instead of the most polarizing figure in American politics, she was the most popular governor in America, boasting an approval rating that had been as high as 93 percent in a state where Independents outnumber Republicans or Democrats. She had earned a reputation as a courageous reformer, taking on the corrupt Alaskan Republican political machine. Her most pronounced policy expertise was in the broadly popular area of energy independence, and she sounded themes designed to appeal to independent voters: "This is a moment when principles and political independence matter a lot more than just the party line." She checked all the basic boxes when it came to the social conservative litmus tests, but they did not seem to define her. And no one was going to confuse her with Dick Cheney.

Questions about her political ability evaporated after her nomination speech in Minneapolis—an instant classic written by Matthew Scully, a former Bush speechwriter and book-length defender of vegetarianism (an odd pairing with the newly famous moose hunter)—was rapturously received by the conservative crowd. Here was a formidable talent, able to smile while sliding in a rhetorical knife, the newest symbol of small-town values squaring off against the liberal elite—Spiro Agnew in a dress.

But the combination of one of the least nationally known picks in history, paired with the oldest nominee in history, had reporters—and opposition researchers—

furiously doing their due diligence into the woman who could have been one chicken bone away from the presidency. The Republican spin room seemed prepared.

"The media doesn't understand getting up at 3 a.m. to hunt a moose; they don't understand eating a mooseburger,"[2] said Florida Representative Adam Putnam in an awkward attempt to pre-empt liberal media bias. It wasn't the mooseburgers that would cause the trouble.

Problems began when some of her more socially conservative policy positions were unearthed—like opposition to abortion even in the cases of rape and incest (a detail that had not been known by the McCain campaign senior policy staff). Then it came to light that her seventeen-year-old daughter, Bristol, was pregnant, unmarried and keeping the baby.

This news had the unexpected effect of helping Sarah Palin hit the pro-life trifecta, with a special-needs baby (the governor had given birth to a son with Down syndrome four months before), a perfect pro-life record and an unmarried pregnant daughter carrying her child to term while in high school. If a Democratic nominee had a pregnant teenage daughter, reflexive family values attacks might have been deafening—this was the party that two decades before had pilloried Candice Bergen's television character Murphy Brown for having a fictional child out of wedlock because it set a bad example for the nation. But now the same social conservative voices who weeks before had been tut-tutting over the teenage pregnancy of tween idol Jamie Lynn Spears

found a bracing honesty and integrity in Bristol's situa-
tion, evidence of a real American family that folks could
relate to. (It should be remembered that the media feeding frenzy was stopped by none other than Barack
Obama, who simply stated to reporters one disarming
fact: "My mother had me when she was 18.")

Palin quickly became a lightning rod for the left. The
netroots took their ideological opposition and added
tabloid attacks that aimed at her family. Feminist icons
like Gloria Steinem attacked her for representing the
wrong kind of change. It was reminiscent of the anger
directed at Clarence Thomas after the first President
Bush tapped him to succeed Thurgood Marshall on the
Supreme Court. Not just his qualifications for the office,
but the legitimacy of his voice for African-Americans
was at issue. Palin was the same kind of apostate—in
this case, a traitor to her gender.

All of which made her more beloved to conservatives.
As long as all the social conservative and fiscal conservative litmus tests are met, they will not hesitate to rush
to the defense of a fellow traveler who is under attack
from the liberal media. It is both a sport and a pastime.
And with Palin, they were defending a lady's honor,
which is always worth an extra dose of moral outrage.

But the woman nicknamed "Sarah Barracuda" by her
high school basketball team was no shrinking violet.
She reveled in the traditional VP nominee attack-dog
role, delivering most of the memorable sound bites from
the GOP team:

- "Our opponent is someone who sees America as being so imperfect that he's palling around with terrorists who would target their own country. . . . This is not a man who sees America as you see America and as I see America."[3]
- "We believe that the best of America is in these small towns that we get to visit, and in these wonderful little pockets of what I call the real America, being here with all of you hard working very patriotic, very pro-America areas of this great nation."[4]
- "Barack Obama calls it 'spreading the wealth,' Joe Biden calls higher taxes patriotic, but Joe the Plumber and Ed the Dairy Man, I believe that they think that it sounds more like socialism. . . . Friends, now is no time to experiment with socialism."[5]

They were more the tone of talk radio than someone on a presidential ticket, but that was the key to their resonance. Just as with a talk radio host hammering home a point, there was no such thing as too extreme: the more outrageous, the more memorable and therefore the more effective. Their accuracy or broader impact was unimportant, an elitist concern. These sound bites not only owned their own news cycle, they ended up metastasizing into the body politic.

The more populist conservatives loved her, the more liberals loathed her. Tina Fey's impersonation of her on *Saturday Night Live* often simply used Palin's own words as a script. When she epically botched her interviews with Katie Couric, her combination of innate confidence with a disinterest in policy details caused critics to hear echoes of George W. Bush. Her fans saw Ronald Reagan.

But some Reagan-era alumni of the conservative movement were starting to have their doubts. David Brooks pronounced her "a fatal cancer to the Republican Party. . . . Reagan had an immense faith in the power of ideas. But there has been a counter, more populist tradition, which is not only to scorn liberal ideas but to scorn ideas entirely. And I'm afraid that Sarah Palin has those prejudices."[6] Kathleen Parker called on her to resign from the VP slot to "save McCain, her party, and the country she loves."[7] They weren't the only ones: McCain staffers were starting to spew out their regrets in the press, accusing her of "playing for her own future" as a party leader and potential presidential candidate. Palin saw herself "as the beginning and end of all wisdom," vented another.[8]

No matter. Out in "real America," Palin was the star on the circuit, drawing crowds that sometimes outnumbered the top of the ticket. She was relatable and relevant, a symbol of comforting change compelling almost spooky devotion. At a rally in Ohio, one teenage supporter offered a contrast between Obama and Palin: "He seems like a sheep, or a wolf in sheep's clothing to be honest with you. And I believe Palin, she is filled with the Holy Spirit and I believe she will bring honesty and integrity to the White House."[9]

Sarah Palin wasn't just polarizing the electorate, she

was polarizing the Republican Party, driving a wedge
between populists and centrists. Some hard-core conservatives who had long disliked McCain's unpredictable
independence—his co-authoring of legislation with
Democrats like his friend and supporter Joe Lieberman—went to the polls because of Palin. "John McCain
was not our guy," explained David Kelly. "McCain is Republican in Name Only—too much of the moderate
views of leaning towards the middle. . . . When I voted I
had to hold my nose because had McCain not picked
Sarah Palin I would not have voted for the Republican
Party candidate personally."

For all her success at energizing the base, there was
evidence Palin was losing more votes than she was at-
tracting. By the end of October 2008, 59 percent of
American voters believed that Sarah Palin was not ready
for the job,[10] and 47 percent of centrists said they were
less likely to vote for McCain because of Palin's presence
on the ticket.[11] And oddly, while she was supposed to
attract women to the GOP, Palin was less popular with
women than men.[12]

Nonetheless, after the election, the Palin star was
undimmed among the true believers. She didn't attend
the Conservative Political Action Committee conference
in February '09, but she was well represented. Buttons
and bumper stickers saying, "Don't blame me, I voted
for Sarah" were pinned and plastered on unlikely surfaces, her face poked out of pamphlets and posters.
Competing Draft Palin organizations were in attendance,

including Team Sarah, whose Web site had rolled right over from supporting her in the '08 campaign to priming for 2012. A look into the comments on their Web site revealed a combination of adulation ("Most people (like the media) who try to make others believe that Sara is dumb and stupid or inexperienced actually fear her because of her faith and goodness.") and Obama Derangement Syndrome. One post caught my eye because of the fury it directed at someone conjured up as the anti-Palin, First Lady Michelle Obama: "I have never actually HATED anyone in politics before now. . . . She is stupid, mean, power hungry, manipulative, corrupt, essentially ignorant—a poster girl for Institutionalized Black Racism and Agression [sic], a take-no-prisoners warrior for Political Correctnes [sic] aka Socialist Realism and a racially driven Communist fellow traveller. Let her go run an African country. She doesn't fit in here with the American People."[13]

Through the spring's Tea Parties, Palin was in Alaska, but her absence made the heart grow fonder. For all the attempts of presidential hopefuls like Mike Huckabee and Newt Gingrich to ride that wave, Palin was the most popular by far, rivaling even Reagan for references on signs and T-shirts. She was becoming the conservative answer to Obama—a symbol of hope and change for conservatives.

After abruptly resigning from office to "not retreat but reload," Palin communicated to her masses via Facebook and Twitter ("I don't have to go through the mainstream media . . . spinning my words") firing off policy dispatches and personal updates while writing her multi-million dollar memoirs.

Without any organized effort or op-eds, her post alleging Obama's "death panels" single-handedly moved the summer's health-care debate and drove the tone of the town halls. It was a compact Wingnut classic, combining self-referential patriotism with apocalyptic big government imagery and a threatened baby, to boot. "The America I know and love is not one in which my parents or my baby with Down syndrome will have to stand in front of Obama's 'death panel' so his bureaucrats can decide, based on a subjective judgment of their 'level of productivity in society,' whether they are worthy of health care. Such a system is downright evil."[14]

Here again the talk radio model was proving its effectiveness—if you throw a bomb, people take notice. And when criticism came, it could be dismissed as just the liberal media knocking her again. Defenders would come. There would be no apologies, and Sarah's army loved it that way.

Palin's support was deep but not broad. With approval ratings north of 80 percent among Republicans, her disapproval ratings are just as high among Democrats. And 58 percent of independents believed she did not understand "complex issues." Given Palin's increasingly public professions of her Christian faith on the political stage—and the news that she believed her nomination for vice president was "God's Plan"—it's perhaps not surprising that her strongest support comes from white evangelical protestants, regular churchgoers, and the self-described "very conservative."

But Palin is also hugely popular with the talk radio crowd, especially fans of Rush Limbaugh. Forty-eight percent of Limbaugh's listeners say that Palin best represents Republican's core values out of all likely party leaders in 2012 while 45 percent said they would vote for her in their state's presidential primary.[15]

As it turns out, the Birthers are also big fans—66 percent of those who believe that Barack Obama may not have been born in the United States say that Sarah Palin is their favorite out of the likely 2012 presidential pack.[16] And when Palin subsequently was asked about Obama's birth certificate on the Rusty Humphries radio show, she offered just enough encouragement to keep those home fires burning. "I think the public, rightfully, is still making it an issue. I don't have a problem with that. I don't know if I would have to bother to make it an issue, because I think enough members of the electorate still want answers."[17]

Sarah Palin fans are so eager for 2012 that they offer up vice presidential candidates on signs at rallies and on Web sites, reflecting their vision of a Wingnut dream team. A Palin-Beck ticket has been imagined, an outside-the-beltway celebrity duo selling a return to common sense. After Joe Wilson shouted "You lie!" at Obama during a Joint Session of Congress, Palin/Wilson 2012 signs popped up days later at the 9/12 rally.

I asked Adam Brickley, the blogger who successfully started the push to get the McCain campaign to nominate Palin in 2008, what he made of this rush to pair Palin with some of the more angry and uncivil voices in the GOP. "Those people who are hard-core enough to carry a 'You Lie!' sign tend to like bluntness and straight talk and that's what they get from Sarah Palin."

Bluntness and straight talk—no apologies. That's a mantra fitting a Fox News contributor or a radio talk show host. And the big daddy of them all has nothing but good things to say about Sarah Palin: "This woman has far more patriotism and love of country and decency in her than Barack Obama could hope to have. This woman would be so much better leading this country than what we have now because we are being led into destruction. . . .We are being led by a man who's got a chip on his shoulder for some reason about this country and doesn't like it. She loves it."[18]

The Limbaugh Brigades

Rush Limbaugh is the founder of the Wingnut feast. The political entertainer and professional polarizer graced the cover of *Time* magazine as the voice of conservative populism in the wake of the 1994 Republican revolution, and he's been going strong ever since. A generation of conservatives had grown up listening to him trash liberals, the Clintons and "elite, country club Rockefeller Republicans." Social issues, with the exception of abortion, are rarely discussed—he is a man of appetites. Loyal fans are called dittoheads, a label both mocking and encouraging their tendency to fall in line with El Rushbo. The son of Cape Girardeau, Missouri, is now the $400 million man, with the most lucrative contract recorded in any medium, reaching twenty million people a week.[19]

But there's a secret beneath those numbers that reflects the Republican Party's broader problem—nearly half of Rush's listeners are over sixty-five.[20] While he's got favorable ratings from 60 percent of Republicans, only 25 percent of independents and 6 percent of Democrats agree.[21] Unlike Republicans, Rush can afford not to care.

After the 2008 election, Rush dubbed himself "the last man standing." In the lead-up to inauguration, a magazine asked Rush to write 400 words on his hopes for the Obama administration. "I don't need 400 words," he told his audience. "I need four: 'I hope he fails.'"[22]

His opposition to Obama was alternately philosophic—seminars about the virtues of conservatism versus the evils of liberalism—and just plain weird. "We are being told that we have to hope he succeeds, that we have to bend over, grab the ankles, bend over forward, backward, whichever, because his father was black, because this is the first black president."[23]

As long as Rush was in the news, it was good for ratings. And the Obama administration initially liked it that way. In a "don't throw me in that brier patch" moment, chief of staff Rahm Emanuel said that Limbaugh was "the voice and the intellectual force and energy behind the Republican Party."[24] It was a contrast that worked to their advantage.

When newly elected RNC Chair Michael Steele was asked whether Rush was the de facto head of the GOP, he said "Rush Limbaugh is an entertainer" and described his style as "incendiary" and "ugly." The blowback among the base was so great that he was compelled to engage in an extended grovel of an apology. "I have enormous respect for Rush Limbaugh," Steele told Politico. "I went back at that tape and I realized words that I said weren't what I was thinking. . . . I wasn't trying to slam him or anything."[25] When he tried to phone in an apology Rush did not immediately take the call.

Rush Limbaugh has political power without responsibilities. He does not need to worry about governing or winning elections, only keeping his audience engaged and enraged. He uses conflict, tension and resentment to increase his ratings. And his influence has inspired a new generation of Wingnut politicians who are choosing to follow the narrow but intense popularity of his model.

These are the Limbaugh Brigades.

In the past, they might have been blocked from office for being too extreme. But the rigged system of redistricting has helped push political power to the margins. The creation of safe seats has resulted in a 96 percent re-election rate,[26] effectively ending competitive general elections. That makes the only real contest a partisan primary—and if only 10 percent of the electorate turns out, 5.1 percent makes a majority. It's a paradise for activists, empowering ideological warriors who do not have to worry about winning voters in the center of the political spectrum. Instead, they can focus on playing to the base.

Their extreme politics makes them popular in their party but deeply polarizing figures to the electorate-at-large—just like Limbaugh.

The more angry and unhinged their claims, the more they are celebrated as courageous by activists in the base—just like Limbaugh.

Minnesota Congresswoman Michele Bachmann is a prime example. Elected to Congress in 2006, after she told supporters God called on her to run, Michele first made a national name for herself by declaring that Obama "may have anti-American views"—and calling for an investigation of other Democrats with "anti-American" views in October of 2008[27]—the media fall-out casting Bachmann as a neo-McCarthy made her, if anything, more beloved by conservatives.

She continued with a string of howlers and incite-ments in the first year of the Obama administration. On Cap and Trade, she urged Minnesotans to be "armed and dangerous on this issue of the energy tax because we need to fight back."[28] She opposed funding for AmeriCorps, saying she foresaw "a very strong chance that we will see that young people will be put into mandatory service" with "re-education camps"[29] (her son later voluntarily enlisted). On health care she urged an audience: "What we have to do today is make a covenant, to slit our wrists, be blood brothers on this thing. This will not pass. . . . Right now, we are looking at reaching down the throat and ripping the guts out of freedom."[30] She's called for an "orderly revolution," saying that "where tyranny is enforced upon the people, as Barack Obama is doing, the people suffer and mourn."[31] The media covers her because she makes great copy, and conservative populists love her because they think she's talking truth to power.

Texas Congressman Louie Gohmert was an early adopter of the "Kill Granny" arguments against health-care reform, proclaiming "this socialist health care . . . is going to absolutely kill senior citizens. They'll put them on lists and force them to die early."[32] He took to the House floor to argue against the hate crimes bill, saying if gays and lesbians were covered by the bill, then "if you're oriented toward animals, bestiality, then that's not something that could be held against you . . . which means that you'd have to strike any laws against bestiality. If you're oriented toward corpses, toward children. You know, there are all kinds of perversions, some would say it sounds like fun, but most of us would say were perversions . . . and there have been laws against them and this bill says that whatever you're oriented toward sexually that cannot be a source of bias against someone."[33] He is also one of the eleven co-sponsors of the Birther bill in Congress with over 60 percent of the vote. First elected to his safe seat in '04, he has been re-elected.

Iowa Congressman Steve King earned a rebuke from
John McCain in 2008 when he said that if Obama "is
elected president, then the radical Islamists, the al-
Qaida, the radical Islamists and their supporters, will be
dancing in the streets in greater numbers than they did
on September 11 because they will declare victory in
this War on Terror."[34] He raised eyebrows as the only
member of Congress to not vote for a resolution ac-
knowledging the use of slave labor in the construction
of the U.S. Capitol Building. In response to the "day
without an immigrant" protests, King wrote in an op-ed
for his local paper, "The lives of 12 U.S. citizens would
be saved who otherwise die a violent death at the hands
of murderous illegal aliens each day. . . . Eight American
children would not suffer the horror as a victim of a sex
crime."[35] And when commenting on Representative Joe
Wilson, King argued that "The President threw the first
punch" and then called Wilson "an officer and a gentle-
man and a patriot." "God bless him," King said. "He
said what we were thinking."[36]

It is not just happening on the right. Increasingly,
Wingnuts on the left are pursuing elected office with an
angry activist mindset, a reflexive mirror of the forces
that Limbaugh unleashed. In 2009, freshman Florida
Democratic Representative Alan Grayson went on a
search for hyper-partisan accolades as he tried to label
himself "the congressman with guts." In a speech on the
House floor, he said, "The Republican health care plan is
this: 'Don't get sick, and if you do get sick, die quickly.'"

Days later he attacked Republicans as "foot-dragging, knuckle-dragging Neanderthals who think they can dictate policy to America by being stubborn." That was mild compared to what came next: calling Republicans "the enemy of America" and "certainly the enemy of peace."[37] He rounded out the diatribes by calling an aide to Fed Chair Ben Bernanke a "K-Street Whore" on 9/11 Truther Alex Jones's radio show. Here's what was most impressive: Grayson made all these comments in the space of one month.[38] Even more impressive was the tough-talking congressman's sensitivity to criticism. When a Florida resident from a neighboring district created a Web site titled mycongressmanisnuts.com, Grayson wrote a letter to U.S. Attorney General Eric Holder accusing the site of lying and being "utterly tasteless" as well as "juvenile." He concluded by asking that his critic be put in jail for five years.[39] Seriously.

This culture of unhinged commentary from the conservative Limbaugh Brigades may have been crystallized when Joe Wilson shouted, "You Lie!" But Wilson's outburst was soon outdone by Arizona Congressman Trent Franks's remark that President Obama "has no place in any station of government and we need to realize that he is an enemy of humanity."[40]

"An enemy of humanity"—let that roll off your tongue for a while. It's hard to find a more global a condemnation than that—and yet the comment was brushed aside as overheated and unremarkable, just one more conservative getting carried away by playing to the base.

Congressman Franks offered his impassioned rant in front of the How to Take Back America Conference, hosted in St. Louis by Wingnut matriarch Phyllis Schlafly ("Feminism is the most destructive force in the world") and WorldNetDaily columnist Janet Folger Porter.

To get a taste of the Take Back America crowd, take a look at some of the workshops offered to attendees: "How to counter the homosexual extremist movement," "How to defeat UN attacks on sovereignty," "How to Stop Feminist and Gay Attacks on the Military" and, inevitably, "How to recognize living under Nazis & Communists." A companion DVD featuring a shadowy Hitler-like figure plotting a takeover of the U.S.A. was for sale under the title "Freedom to Dictatorship in 5 Years."

Given this lunatic fringe festival, you might imagine that few elected officials would attend for fear of guilt by association. But as you might have guessed by now, you'd be wrong.

Once and future presidential candidate Mike Huckabee had taken time from his Fox News TV and radio show to give the keynote speech, railing against the U.N.: "It's time to get a jackhammer and to simply chip off that part of New York City and let it float into the

East River, never to be seen again!"[41] After he spoke a power-point offered these parting wishes: "Where would America be today if Gov. Huckabee were President Huckabee? We sure wouldn't be celebrating Ramadan . . . Huckabee 2012."[42]

Michele Bachmann brought the crowd to its feet by decrying the "gangster government" that was now running the White House, an alliterative riff off the "thugocracy" conservatives had predicted.[43] She spoke of the dangers of a "one-world currency" and advocated defense of "American sovereignty, even if President Obama's czars want to give it away."[44] And she promised that if Republicans took back Congress in 2010 "defunding the left is going to be so easy and it's going to solve so many of our problems."[45]

Steve King was on hand to present Joe the Plumber with the coveted Golden Wrench Award ("for throwing a wrench in the works") and a Golden Plunger ("to help flush out Washington"). King told the crowd, "I ran for public office because of what the government was doing to us, not because of what I wanted the government to do for us," and warned that in the effort to stop liberals "every conversation matters; every prayer matters; every Tea Party matters."[46]

Conservative blogger and convention speaker Brian Camenker of MassResistance pronounced it "the best conference of its kind in memory. It was God and country—and unflinching, refreshing non-politically-correct sanity."[47]

The How to Take Back America Conference may have been extreme, but it was not an exception.

One week before in Washington's art deco Omni Shoreham Hotel, the Value Voters Summit had convened its high-powered but closed-to-the-press conservative cattle call. The usual suspects all appeared—including Huckabee and Bachmann—but they were joined by presidential hopefuls Mitt Romney, Newt Gingrich and Minnesota Governor Tim Pawlenty. There were religious figures ranging from the Family Research Council's Tony Perkins to born-again B-movie actor Stephen Baldwin. And rounding things out was former Miss California-turned-conservative-sex-symbol Carrie Prejean, a martyr to the liberal media for support of what she called "opposite marriage" as opposed to same-sex marriage.

The How to Take Back America themes were in full force, with breakout sessions titled "Thugocracy: Fighting the Vast Left-Wing Conspiracy" and "ObamaCare: Rationing Your Life Away." Minority Whip Eric Cantor got in touch with his inner Glenn Beck by saying, "Right now, millions of Americans are waking up realizing that they don't recognize their country anymore." During Mitt Romney's address an audience member channeled Joe Wilson and shouted "He lies!" to which Mitt quipped, "I approve of that comment."[48]

But it was the Huckster who walked away the event's big winner with a speech rejecting calls to modernize or moderate the party. "I'm not sure the center makes a whole lot of sense when it's coming from people who

certainly don't have our interest, or our country's interest, at heart."[49] This was a new assault—saying that
centrist Republicans were not just trying to subvert the
GOP, but that they "certainly" did not have America's
best interest at heart. It was the kind of attack that had
previously been directed at liberals, but now the enemy's list was growing to include all but the true believers. These appeals helped the ordained minister and
former Arkansas governor win the Values Voters straw
poll easily, apparently answering the question the title
of one book for sale in the hall asked: "Who Would Jesus Vote For?"

Beneath the heartfelt talk of God and Country there is
a strangeness seeping into our politics, not just incivility but outright hostility. It is a sign of the increasing influence of the extremes, embracing the slash-and-burn
techniques of a talk radio entertainer instead of the
coalition-building skills of political leaders. But by en-
abling the extremes, Republicans may be sowing the
seeds of their own destruction.

Year-end polls in 2009 showed a hypothetical Tea
Party beating Republicans in a three-way match-up
against Democrats. These fueled conservative populists'
claims to represent an independent third-party movement, reflecting the rise of independent voters to more
than 40 percent of the electorate. There's only one problem: The would-be leaders of the conservative populist
movement hail from the right wing of the Republican
Party. Sarah Palin's popularity is astronomical among

Republicans and conservatives, but she is decidedly unpopular with independents and centrists. Likewise,
Rush Limbaugh is hugely popular with conservatives
and Republicans, but his brand of harsh partisanship is
kryptonite to independents and centrists. The source of
this disconnect is not a mystery. A 2008 survey by
TargetPoint Consulting found that 96 percent of centrist
voters consider themselves conservative to moderate on
fiscal issues, while 86 percent of centrists see themselves
as liberal to moderate on social issues. To put it another
way, only 4 percent of centrists describe themselves as
fiscal liberals while just 14 percent describe themselves
as social conservatives. The rise of independent voters
has been in reaction to the increased polarization of the
two parties, while conservative populists believe that
the parties are not polarized *enough*. For all the libertarian talk, the only independence their leaders advocate is
moving further to the right on social as well as fiscal issues. Conservative populists' threats to bolt from the
Republican Party may not be a bluff, but they are an attempt to hold the GOP hostage to its most fundamentalist elements, hijacking American politics in the process.
You cannot unite a country by first trying to divide it.

HUNTING FOR HERETICS

In 2008, the most competitive Senate race was in Minnesota between Al Franken—the longtime *Saturday Night Live* comic, liberal Air America host and author of best sellers like *Rush Limbaugh Is a Big Fat Idiot*—and the incumbent Republican Senator Norm Coleman, a one-time Woodstock attendee turned prosecutor and the former mayor of St. Paul. While Obama won the state by 10 percent, Coleman's broad center-right profile helped him gain enough crossover votes to make the race too close to call, with a gap of 0.01 percent—or 225 votes out of the 2.9 million cast.

But the morning after the election, some Wingnuts on the right were calling for Coleman's defeat. Here's the logic of young conservative radio host Ben Ferguson: "I think a lot of people last night think this was a cleansing for the party. We got rid of some dead weight, we got rid of some RINOS—Republicans In Name Only. There are Republicans today, like myself, that are rooting against Norm Coleman, hoping Al Franken wins, just so we can at least have a real Republican next time around. I mean, for me I'm like 'Let's kick 'em all out,' you know. The ones that act like they're real conservatives that weren't, hey, go on home."[1]

Ferguson eventually got his wish. Eight months later,

the Minnesota Supreme Court rejected Coleman's appeal and the Senate Democratic caucus got precisely the sixty votes it needed to beat back a filibuster, the tactic Republicans had counted on to check Obama's agenda.

The convictions that led some Wingnut conservatives to find a paradoxical satisfaction in defeat were neatly expressed by a sign I saw paraded at the Tea Partiers' 9/12 march on Washington: "All progressive or liberal democrats or republicans are communists." They are not interested in rebuilding the Republican Party if it means forming coalitions with anyone who is not a strict social conservative as well as a fiscal conservative. They want to see the party purged, Stalinist-style, before it rebuilds—even if it means being defeated by Democrats. It's an inquisition based on ideological purity. Conformity is courage. Dissent is disloyal.

Centrist Republicans are targeted by conservative groups like the Club for Growth, which run right-wing candidates in closed primaries who win and then often promptly lose the general election to Democrats. In 2006 and 2008, such self-inflicted losses included Representatives Heather Wilson and Wayne Gilchrest. "They don't make any bones about losing elections so long as they purify the party," said Senator Arlen Specter, who abandoned the GOP ship after twenty-four years in the face of a tough primary challenge from Club for Growth President Pat Toomey. "I don't understand it. . . . There ought to be an outcry."[2]

The latest example came in a 2009 special election for

an upstate New York congressional seat that had been held by Republicans since 1872. It was won by a Democrat because the Wingnuts split the right. New York State Conservative Party candidate Doug Hoffman challenged local Republican elected official Dede Scozzafava, drawing national support from Sarah Palin and conservative pundits who characterized the GOP nominee as a "radical leftist" because she was pro-choice and pro-gay marriage. Brian Brown, executive director of the National Organization for Marriage, made his intentions clear: "The Republican Party cannot take someone as liberal as Dede Scozzafava and thrust her out on the voters and expect the voters just to accept it."

"You can have a very, very intense movement of 20 percent. You can't govern,"[3] Newt Gingrich cautioned a week before the election, explaining his support for the party nominee. "To govern, you got to get 50 percent plus one."[3] And for that bit of pragmatic math, the leader of the 1994 Republican revolution was dubbed "King of the RINOS" by the Wingnut netroots.[4]

Soon after this election debacle, a ten-point party-purity petition was advanced by members of the Republican National Committee, proposing that any candidate who broke with conservatives on three or more of these issues—in any votes, public statements or on a questionnaire—would be denied party funds or the party endorsement.[5]

There is a struggle going on between the 50 staters and the 51 percenters—those who want a broad, diverse and national Republican Party against those who are content to only play to the base in pursuit of narrow victories. Right now, the 51 percenters seem to be winning. The hunt for heretics has helped make congressional Republicans extinct in an entire region. In 1997, the Club for Growth's Stephen Moore published an article in the *American Spectator* titled "Is the Northeast Necessary?" in which he suggested Republicans should "[write] off this dying region once and for all."[6] Twelve years later, Moore had gotten his wish. There isn't a single Republican representative left in all of New England. This is what success looks like in the all-or-nothing world of the RINO hunters.

There is a special fury inside the conservative movement directed at Republicans who don't walk in lockstep with both social and fiscal conservatives. The goal of the RINO hunters is spelled out on the Web site of conservative activist Bob MacGuffie at Right Principles: "The RINO is a destructive animal that tramples on many people's hard work. It has no useful objective in an American sense because it feeds on destruction of our individual liberties and freedoms. It is a parasite that needs to be driven into political extinction!"[7]

Abraham Lincoln and Teddy Roosevelt are dubbed RINOs (because they were "progressive plutocrats"), and the site goes on to offer a RINO hit list, including Senators John McCain, Richard Lugar, Lindsey Graham, Kit Bond, Lamar Alexander, Mel Martinez, Judd Gregg, Susan Collins and Olympia Snowe. Among the Representatives mentioned are Mark Kirk, Jeff Flake, Mike Castle, Mary Bono Mack, David Reichert, John McHugh, Chris Smith and John Sullivan.

John McCain—a pro-life, fiscal conservative war hero—has been a target of RINO hunters over the years because of his political independence and willingness to criticize both conservative and liberal excesses. After the election, when McCain's daughter Meghan began advocating on The Daily Beast and television that the party should modernize itself on issues like gay rights, she became a target of Wingnut familial suspicions. When Arlen Specter defected, Rush Limbaugh invited the GOP's recent nominee to do the same: "Take McCain and his daughter with you."

We've seen the hunt for heretics before.

During the southern conservative "massive resistance" to desegregation, moderate critics were derided as traitors, double-crossers, sugar-coated integrationists and cowards.[8]

During the anticommunist heyday of Joe McCarthy and the John Birch Society, a new umbrella term was introduced, "ComSymp"—for "communist sympathizer"— that allowed any skeptic to be stigmatized without the difficulty of actually proving they were communist. At the time, Republican Senator Milton R. Young of North Dakota reflected on the Birchers' obsession with what would become known as RINO hunting: "Strangely

enough, most of the criticism is leveled not against liberal public officials but against more middle of the road,
and even conservative Republicans."[9]

And while Nixon VP Spiro Agnew invented the use
of the word "squish" to refer to radical liberals in the
late '60s and early '70s, by the Reagan revolution it was
used by conservatives to denigrate centrist members of
their own party, notably Reagan chief of staff (and future secretary of state) James Baker and then–Vice President George H. W. Bush.[10]

But the hyper-partisan hunt for heretics really got
mainstreamed during the administration of the second
Bush. At the outset, conservative activist Grover
Norquist gleefully told Pat Robertson's 700 Club that
"there isn't an 'us and them' with this administration.
They is us. We is them."[11]

Poisonous partisanship got a new name in the later
part of the Bush administration when the actions of
Monica Goodling came to light. Goodling was the
thirty-four-year-old Justice Department White House
liaison—known as "she who must be obeyed" by her
staff—who illegally imposed partisan social conservative litmus tests on prospective Justice Department civil
service employees.

An investigation found that Goodling—a graduate of
Messiah College and Pat Robertson's Regent Law
School—asked about abortion in thirty-four interviews
and gay marriage on at least twenty-one different occa-
sions.[12] She recommended Internet searches be applied

to job applicants to gain insight into their political beliefs, and just before Christmas 2006, Goodling e-mailed political appointee John Nowacki urging him to "hire one more good American"—a phrase he later testified applied exclusively to conservatives.

Even the pioneering secretary of state and Bush loyalist Condoleezza Rice was considered suspect by second-tier administration conservatives because of her position on social issues. When one applicant expressed admiration for Condoleezza Rice, Goodling frowned and said, "But she is pro-choice."[13]

Over the course of the Bush administration, but especially during the 2008 election, the excommunications and defections continued. Individuals who were once considered among the brightest young minds of the Reagan and Thatcher era have been caught up in this dragnet—Peggy Noonan, David Frum, David Brooks and Andrew Sullivan—each declaring their independence to differing degrees and receiving a hailstorm of right-wing criticism in return. Some might argue—as Reagan once did about the Democrats—that they didn't leave the party, the party had left them. But this was not the time or place for debating differences of opinion.

The son of William F. Buckley, Jr., waded into the crossfire by endorsing Barack Obama for president after the Palin nomination. Chris Buckley chose The Daily Beast as the location of the announcement instead of the *National Review,* founded by his father, because "I don't have the kidney at the moment for 12,000 e-mails saying how good it is he's no longer alive to see his Judas of a son endorse for the presidency a covert Muslim who pals around with the Weather Underground."[14] He got his 12,000 angry e-mails any way.

Buckley—who describes his politics as that of "a small-government conservative who clings tenaciously and old-fashionedly to the idea that one ought to have balanced budgets. On abortion, gay marriage, *et al.*, I'm libertarian"—found himself no longer welcome in the pages of the magazine his father founded.

When David Frum—another *National Review* alum and a former George W. speechwriter—engaged in a public debate with Rush Limbaugh over the future direction of the GOP, he was barraged with angry e-mails from dittoheads. "Most of these e-mails say some version of the same thing: if you don't agree with Rush, quit calling yourself a conservative and get out of the Republican Party. There's the perfect culmination of the outlook Rush Limbaugh has taught his fans and followers: We want to transform the party of Lincoln, Eisenhower and Reagan into a party of unanimous dittoheads—and we don't care how much the party has to shrink to do it. That's not the language of politics. It's the language of a cult."[15]

The cult-like impulse to hunt for heretics has only escalated. The founder of the acclaimed blog LittleGreen Footballs.com, Charles Johnson, got his first big boost railing against Islamist radicalism after the attacks of 9/11. But in the Bush administration's second term, he started to criticize excesses from the far right as well—taking aim at creationism and the increased influence of the religious right.

"I've been pretty much labeled as a heretic now by all the people who used to be what I would consider friends and allies," Johnson told me. "I'm getting more hate mail nowadays than I got even at the height of my popularity as an anti-Jihadist, which was very surprising to me, because I used to get some pretty nasty hate mail from radical Islamists. But the stuff I'm getting right now from right-wingers is an order of magnitude worse."[16]

When it comes to seeing an order of magnitude worse up close, you're not going to outdo what you're about to see from the inbox of nationally syndicated columnist Kathleen Parker.

In late September of 2008, Parker had the temerity to criticize Sarah Palin in the pages of *National Review*, concluding after a month of watching that the Alaskan VP nominee was "out of her league." "No one hates saying that more than I do," she wrote: "Like so many women, I've been pulling for Palin, wishing her the best, hoping she will perform brilliantly. I've also noticed that I watch her interviews with the held breath of an anxious parent, my finger poised over the mute button in case it gets too painful. Unfortunately, it often does. My cringe reflex is exhausted."[17]

Within a week she'd gotten 11,000 e-mails. By week three the total passed 20,000. She estimates that about

70 percent were negative, with the general theme being that she was a traitor.

"I didn't realize that I worked for the GOP," says Kathleen, "or that my job as a 'conservative' columnist meant I had to defend all things Republican."[18]

Here are some choice cuts from her e-mail bag at the time:

- "You're not one of us, you're one of THEM, the liberal lovers, the flag burners, country haters, the ones who want to kill god and put Stalin in his place and see this nation destroyed by a sea of brown people and gays. Do you secretly date black men, Parker? You make me sick you sickening sick witch!!!"
- "So the republican party is supposed to surrender their traditional values in order to expand the base. Have you always been a dumb, trashy cunt or did sucking Obama's schlong fill your head with such bull-shit that you can't even think straight."
- "You're a fucking, shit-faced whore and you are the reason for the decline of the republican party. Yes. You and every pansy shit-headed fucking liberal republican who caters to the leftist agenda."
- "You like getting cucumbers up your ass, whore? Huh? Stop writing your stupid articles. Conservative Christians don't like you and your ilk, we don't need you or your fucking ideas. We will do fine without republicans, democrats, or anyone else who tries to disregard our values."

- "Kathleen Parker is a lesbian, anti-christian whore and anti-American terrorist who must be eradicated. She is an Adolph [sic] Hitler of this century."

There is something breathtakingly stupid about seeing such bile written down instead of just hearing it screamed. For some unhinged hyper-partisans, a hint of dissent provokes unreasonable rage. When thoughtful criticism is responded to with an avalanche of hate, its absurdity is the only saving grace.

You don't want to indulge in close readings of deranged right-wing dispatches like a high school class reading *Hamlet*, but in those five e-mails you get the whole gamut of paranoid associations—Hitler, Stalin, people who "want to kill God," "Us versus Them," and fear of the nation being "destroyed by a sea of brown people and gays"—a two-fer of racism and homophobia. What's especially weird is the abrupt segues between high-minded conservative arguments and then the slide into the psychotic sewer.

Hunting for heretics pretends to be a principled fight for ideological purity, but behind that mask is an uglier impulse, an attempt to intimidate and insist on conformity. Imperiousness and inflexibility in politics is a sign of insecurity. It's a reminder of what the Czech dissident-turned-president Vaclav Havel once wrote: "Ideology offers human beings the illusion of dignity and morals while making it easier to part with them."

Burning Down the Big Tent

"I've spent my entire life time separating the Right from the kooks."[19] reflected William F. Buckley, Jr. His friend Ronald Reagan won the White House for conservatives by preaching a "big tent" philosophy—noting as far back as 1967, "The Republican Party, both in [California] and nationally, is a broad party. There is room in our tent for many views; indeed, the divergence of views is one of our strengths"[20]—and reminding activists that an 80 percent friend is not a 20 percent enemy.[21] These axioms echoed Reagan's genial personality, but they were also shrewd politics. In 1984, the tent was big enough to hold 59 percent of the electorate and carry forty-nine states.

But now Wingnuts are trying to burn the big tent down. They have forgotten that the essence of evangelism is winning converts. Reagan's oft-quoted Eleventh Commandment—"Thou shalt not speak ill of another Republican"—is dismissed if the Republican is not considered adequately conservative. Even the term "big tent" itself is regarded as code for liberal subversion.

The tone has come from the top as well as from the grassroots activists. When former Vice President Dick Cheney was asked whether the party should follow the lead of Rush Limbaugh or Colin Powell, he chose the professional polarizer instead of the centrist former secretary of state. "Well, if I had to choose in terms of being a Republican, I'd go with Rush Limbaugh," he said with gravelly dismissiveness while sticking in the shiv. "My take on it was Colin had already left the party. I didn't know he was still a Republican."[22]

Here's the irony of today's ideological purists: Conservatives' greatest patron saints, Barry Goldwater and Ronald Reagan, would never have met the "You're either with us or against us" litmus tests of today's right wing. Not even close.

Goldwater was a small-government libertarian who believed in getting government out of both the board room and the bedroom. On the issue of abortion, Goldwater was frustrated that "a lot of so-called conservatives think I've turned liberal because I believe a woman has a right to an abortion. That's a decision that's up to a pregnant woman, not up to the pope or some dogooders or the religious right."[23] It wasn't a newfound view—his wife co-founded Arizona Planned Parenthood in the 1930s.

On gay rights, Goldwater took a live-and-let-live attitude at odds with the social conservative playbook, saying: "The rights that we have under the Constitution cover anything we want to do, as long as it's not harmful. I can't see any way in the world that being a gay can cause damage to somebody else."[24] Of gays in the military, he famously said, "You don't have to be straight in order to shoot straight."[25]

Goldwater was also wary of the growing influence of the religious right on the Republican Party, taking to the floor of the Senate in 1981 to decry "the religious factions that . . . are trying to force government leaders into following their position 100 percent. . . . I'm frankly sick and tired of the political preachers across this country telling me as a citizen that if I want to be a moral person, I must believe in 'A,' 'B,' 'C,' and 'D.' . . . I will fight them every step of the way if they try to dictate their moral convictions to all Americans in the name of 'conservatism.'"[26]

Goldwater's libertarian instincts would color him a liberal in the eyes of current social conservative power brokers. This paradox, in turn, raises questions about the role and influence of libertarians in the party that so many consider their natural home, especially by contrast to the big-spending Democrats. Nick Gillespie, the editor-in-chief of the libertarian magazine *Reason,* has stated that the split is too obvious to ignore. "The Republicans used to talk about cutting taxes, cutting spending, and cutting regulation," Gillespie told me in the lead-up to the 2006 elections after half a decade of conservative control of Washington. "Now, they only talk about cutting taxes and regulating people's personal lives."[27]

Even the sainted Reagan would come under fire from most in the current Republican Party if his policies were judged absent the hagiography. As governor of California, he signed the nation's most liberal abortion bill into law (an action he later said he regretted). In the 1970s, he opposed California's Proposition 6, the conservative bill backed by Anita Bryant, which would have made it legal to fire gays and lesbians from teaching positions in

What would happen if we eliminated parties

public schools. He raised taxes by a billion dollars to close a budget gap and presided over an increase in the number of state employees by 50,000.[28] Any of these actions could get him disqualified as an untrustworthy conservative or even a dangerous liberal, if he tried to step out on the road to the White House today.

As president, Reagan gave amnesty to illegal aliens in a comprehensive immigration reform. He closed tax loopholes that today would be attacked as raising taxes. He negotiated with the Soviet "evil empire" and withdrew troops from Beirut after a terrorist attack. He worked amiably with Democrats in Congress and constantly courted their constituents, creating the Reagan Democrat. In fact, as early as 1981, coalition conservative activists were complaining about Reagan, with the director of the Conservative Caucus saying, "He sounds like Winston Churchill and acts like Neville Chamberlain,"[29] while the editor of the *Conservative Digest* reached absurdity by writing, "Sometimes I wonder how much of a Reaganite Reagan really is."[30]

Today, Rush Limbaugh and Glenn Beck are among the chief critics of the big-tent philosophy. Beck attacked South Carolina Senator Lindsey Graham for saying the GOP can't be the party of "angry white guys" by sarcastically asking, "Who's left?"[31] How about the 85 percent of Americans who don't identify themselves as "conservative Republicans" or the vast majority of non-white citizens who feel unwelcome in what used to be the Party of Lincoln?

Mike Huckabee appears to be building his prospective 2012 campaign around attacking the very idea of a big tent: "One of the things that concerns me is that in the United States there is real talk of maybe we need to have this big tent and accommodate every view. . . . That will kill the conservative movement."[32]

He's playing to grassroots groups like Connecticut's Right Principles that sum up hostility to the big tent: "How long will they accept the fiction of a party that is a 'Big Tent'? . . . How long will it tolerate being politically debilitated by a disease caused by an internal enemy consisting of a disloyal collection of ideological subversives who are, for all intents and purposes, looking to either mutate its host body beyond all recognition or to kill it outright?"[33]

When RNC chair Michael Steele advocated a more inclusive approach to pro-choice Republicans and increased tolerance for gays and lesbians, the Family Research Council's Tony Perkins countered by saying that if Steele was trying to create a big tent for the GOP, the Republican Party would find that it's nothing but an "empty big tent."[34]

There is a core contradiction at the heart of modern conservatism. The party's proudly stated belief in expanding individual freedom is at odds with the agenda of the religious right. A collectivist streak runs through much of social conservatism—a desire to have the government make decisions for individuals, especially on questions of reproductive and sexual freedom.

There's also a secret hiding in plain sight: The far right is far more loud than powerful. The few big-tent Republicans who are left are among the party's most powerful vote getters, even as they are attacked as politically impotent. John McCain won re-election to the Senate in 2004 with 76 percent of the vote. Olympia Snowe won in liberal Maine with 74 percent of the vote and Dick Lugar won with 87 percent in Indiana during the Democratic year of 2006, while social conservative senator Rick Santorum lost in Pennsylvania with 41 percent. In 2008, Lamar Alexander won re-election with 65 percent in Tennessee while conservative senate minority leader Mitch McConnell squeaked by with 53 percent in neighboring Kentucky. And when talk radio advocated a new conservative coalition based on anti-immigrant fervor, two of the border-state candidates backing that approach, Arizona's J. D. Hayworth and Randy Graf, lost their 2006 congressional campaigns.

Joe Scarborough, former GOP congressman and host of *Morning Joe* on MSNBC, provides a conservative's view on the hunt for heretics.

> I hear these freaks screaming and yelling about how they're the true believers, they're the true conservatives. They're the ones that are going to root out the heretics. . . . It's mad-

ness. These are the same people that took a $155 billion surplus when I left Washington in 2001 and turned it into a $1.5 trillion deficit. These are the same so-called conservatives that took the national debt from $5.7 trillion to $11.5 trillion. So when I hear people say the Republican Party's become too conservative, you know what my answer is: they haven't become too conservative. They've become too radical. They stopped being conservative when it came to spending our money. They stopped being conservative when it came to foreign policy. They stopped being conservative in their rhetoric. They have been radicalized by people who don't know what it means to be a small-government conservative.[35]

National Review editor Rich Lowry looks to the future and tells me, "For decades, the way for the Republican Party to grow was to become more conservative and to draw away conservatives from the Democratic Party. But there are various demographic trends that make the Republicans' job tougher and they've sort of tapped out to a large extent that strategy. So now the growth strategy, I think, has to be something different, not to be less conservative but to ensure conservatism is addressing people's current concerns and anxieties."[36]

For the Republican Party, a return to its historic principles of individual freedom, fiscal responsibility and national security—with renewed consistency—would not only lead to the GOP's political resurgence, it could help unite our nation. But it will require that social conservatives embrace the big tent again—and not treat allies with libertarian opinions on social issues as loyalty suspects or second-class citizens.

However, when you hear the far right invoking the big tent these days it's often because they are being forced to defend the indefensible signs that dot the Tea Party and town hall protests. There is a reluctance to repudiate for fear of dividing or demoralizing their partisan forces. Instead, Joe Wierzbicki, one of the GOP operatives organizing the Tea Party Express, contorted himself to avoid judging the occasionally extremist rhetoric and signs amid his crowds: "People who choose to embrace your message or your movement are not the people that you embrace. They have chosen to embrace you."[37] In other words, the big tent should extend as far to the right as necessary to fire up the base. The real disloyalty is not doing violence to civil society but to criticize a fellow traveler. No one is accountable for the mob they incite. It's a sign that the inmates are running the asylum.

From RINO Hunting to DINO Hunting

While the far right set out to eat their own during Obama's first year in the White House, the far left started to indulge the same impulses. But while the far right's constant drumbeat held that Obama was a socialist, the far left attacked him for not being radical enough.

As with the right, the furor started on the fringes even before the inauguration. In early January 2009, the folks at Revolution Books in Manhattan's Chelsea neighborhood weren't even trying to restrain their disgust with liberal excitement over the president-elect. "A lot of people got taken with Obama," the clerk at the checkout counter grumbled, "but it's just the same Bush program rebranded." Instead of the near-ubiquitous Obama buttons adorning overcoats in that area, Revolution had a window display selling bottles of "Obama-lade" for a buck each. It was an oddly entrepreneurial way for them to make a point. Each plastic bottle's wrapper contained a tiny political screed:

INGREDIENTS: Massacres in Gaza, Rick Warren, escalation of the Afghanistan war, Hillary Clinton, bailout of big business, Rahm Emanuel, blaming Black people for problems the system inflicts on them, "coming together" with those who hate gay people, Robert Gates, whitewashing torture by the Bush regime, and the Patriot Act.

SURGEON GENERAL'S WARNING: Obamalade causes massive loss of life in Iraq, Afghanistan, Palestine, Pakistan and many other countries; continued attacks on Black people, women, immigrants, gays & lesbians; political cowardice that is dangerous to the health of humanity. If, after drinking Obamalade, you find yourself accepting the crimes of this system—you should immediately take 2 doses of reality and report to the nearest movement of resistance against these crimes.

Peel off the Obamalade wrapper and you'd have a perfect pocket-sized reminder of the far-left Wingnut worldview: America as the world's prime oppressor.

The professional protesters at a group called "The World Can't Wait" weren't too thrilled about the Obama agenda either. They were formed "to repudiate and stop the fascist direction initiated by the Bush Regime." After Inauguration Day '09 they launched "Obama Watch."

The new president's first sin was the choice of evangelist Rick Warren to give the inauguration invocation: "To say that's a bad start would be a colossal understatement," wrote the organization's director Debra Sweet, going on to describe "Warren's overall Christian fascist program."[38]

Nor were they willing to make adjustments in the oft-cited struggle against the racist imperialism of the U.S.A.: "Having a Black man at the head of a white supremacist government doesn't mean that white supremacy is over!"[39] *Hasta la victoria siempre.*

But the biggest criticism was reserved for Obama's continuation of what they call "the War OF Terror." Here the list of grievances is long: U.S. troops still in Iraq, an expansion of the war against the Taliban in Afghanistan, striking at targets in Pakistan and support for what they call Israel's "occupation" of Gaza. Guantánamo is still open, rendition still practiced and as for torture, well, they're selling stickers with an Abu

Ghraib silhouette over the Obama campaign logo saying, "Yes We Can Cover Up Torture."[40]

As Obama's realpolitik agenda—a surge for Afghanistan, a cautious exit from Guantánamo, pragmatism on health care—began to clash with left-Wingnut ideals, Obamalade fervor began leaking into more mainstream voices.

"Right now, Mr. President, your base thinks you're nothing but a sellout—a corporate sellout at that," bellowed MSNBC's Ed Schultz.[41] "Can you really say this White House is on the side of the American people?" asked Arianna Huffington.[42] Obama, they complained, was too quick to compromise, too eager to horse-trade for a single elusive Republican vote and, most of all, too slow to overturn Bush's foreign policies. The activist Web site Democratic Underground conducted an online poll concluding that Obama was a Democrat in Name Only, while a photo showing Bush's face morphing into Obama's was circulating among the netroots. Some were already suggesting that progressive former presidential candidate Howard Dean challenge Obama in the 2012 primaries.[43] The newly emboldened left was taking on the embattled center. The era of DINO hunting had begun.

Bipartisanship doesn't sell to Wingnuts, left or right. Obama had promised to appoint a "Team of Rivals"–style cabinet if elected, and when he followed through, the Wingnuts weren't happy. Tapping Hillary Clinton to be secretary of state was on the outside edge of acceptable, despite her hawkish positions on the Middle East, but the real news was the selection of former McCain advisor and marine general Jim Jones to be national security advisor and the re-appointment of Bush's secretary of defense, Robert Gates. As the executive director of Moveon.org, Eli Pariser, told the AP: "If they turn out to be all disappointments, we'll have a good three years to storm the gates at the White House."[44] For the far left, the reflexive rhetoric of *Ramparts* always lives on.

With sixty votes in the Senate and a 258-seat majority in the House, liberal leaders viewed Obama's election as an ideological mandate. Congressman Barney Frank quipped, "When Obama said he was going to be a post-partisan president, I got post-partisan depression."[45] Columnist Thomas Franks argued that "bipartisanship is a silly Beltway obsession," writing that "promises to get beyond partisanship are the most perfunctory sort of campaign rhetoric"[46]—trying to absolve Obama of the obligation to govern as he'd campaigned. It was a classic case of situational ethics: Critics of conservative hyper-partisanship couldn't wait to get their equal and opposite revenge.

Each centrist policy enraged the far left even more. On Afghanistan, congressional liberals like Dennis Kucinich reflexively deployed Vietnam metaphors while Bush nemeses like Code Pink took to the streets to protest Obama's "imperialist war against Afghanistan." Even Cindy Sheehan—the self-styled "peace mom" who declared W. a "bigger terrorist than Osama bin Laden"[47]— came out of semi-retirement to protest President Obama on his summer vacation, just like old times: "The body bags aren't taking a vacation and as the U.S.-led violence surges in Afghanistan and Pakistan, so are the needless deaths of every side."[48] She later led protests in Oslo opposite Obama's Nobel Peace Prize acceptance ceremony.[49]

The larger problem for liberals wasn't just Afghanistan but Obama's decision to change the style but not the substance of the Bush administration's War on Terror policies. Obama's expansion of detention for terror suspects spurred nationally syndicated ultra-liberal cartoonist and columnist Ted Rall to erupt in a Wingnut call for Obama's resignation titled "With Democrats Like Him, Who Needs Dictators?": "Obama is useless. Worse than that, he's dangerous. Which is why, if he has any patriotism left after the thousands of meetings he has sat through with corporate contributors, blood-sucking lobbyists and corrupt politicians, he ought to step down now—before he drags us further into the abyss. . . . Obama has revealed himself. He is a monster."[50]

On the domestic front, the Wingnuts turned the health-care debate into a circular firing squad. Moveon .org started targeting centrist Democrats in the Senate with issue ads in their districts, essentially threatening them if they did not back the "public option."[51] The newly formed Progressive Change Campaign Committee aimed to be a liberal corollary to the Club for Growth, targeting ten conservative Blue Dog congressmen for their "Betrayal of Democrats."[52] Joe Lieberman emerged as an especially ripe target for DINO hunters. Al Gore's 2000

VP nominee had emerged as a hawkish "9/11 Democrat." His support of the War on Terror led liberals to successfully primary him with antiwar candidate Ned Lamont in 2006, but Lieberman won the general election as an Independent by 10 percent. Lieberman continued to caucus with the Democrats in the Senate, but he inflamed old wounds by campaigning for John McCain in 2008.

Now with Lieberman a health-care holdout, liberal activists started to play "hunt for the heretic" in exceptionally ugly terms. *Washington Post* blogger Ezra Klein reached for mass murder metaphors, writing, "Lieberman seems primarily motivated by torturing liberals. That is to say, he seems willing to cause the deaths of hundreds of thousands of people in order to settle an old electoral score."[53] Victor Navsky, former editor of the *Nation,* accused Lieberman of "the betrayal of his Jewish heritage."[54] Jesse Jackson also wielded the identity politics machete in an attack on centrist Democrat Congressman Artur Davis of Alabama, saying, "You can't vote against health care and call yourself a black man." Ralph Nader went so far as to call President Obama "an Uncle Tom groveling before the demands of the corporations that are running our country" because the healthcare bill was not liberal enough.

Ultimately, healthcare passed the House and Senate along narrow party lines. This not only failed to fulfill the president's post-partisan campaign promises, it broke with precedent. Every major entitlement expansion or reform in America's past enjoyed broad bipartisan support. FDR's Social Security Act earned the support of 81 House Republicans and 16 GOP senators.[55] LBJ's Medicare Act in 1965 had the support of 70 House Republicans and 13 Senate Republicans.[56] Even the Newt Gingrich–led 1996 Welfare reform enjoyed the support of 98 Democratic votes.[57]

All this Wingnuttery had an impact. Approaching the end of Obama's first year in office, the Democratic-controlled Congress' approval rating was down to 21 percent[58]—lower than President Bush's approval rating when he slunk out of office. They had undercut President Obama's post-partisan promises to such an extent that while he began his term identified with centrist policies, by year-end most Americans saw his agenda as liberal.[59] In November, Democrats lost the governorships of New Jersey and Virginia, swing states Obama carried in 2008. Amid signs that Americans were reverting to their preference for the checks and balances of divided government, liberals were convinced that the problem with their popularity was that they hadn't been liberal enough. The anger erupting from this disconnect was captured in December '09 when Democratic pollster Peter Hart asked a Pennsylvania focus group to write down the word that came to mind when he said "Congress." A retired auto executive named Bill, an independent who had voted for Obama fourteen months before, wrote down "Satan." When Hart asked why, Bill answered, "Because I wasn't sure of the correct spelling of 'Beelzebub.'"[60]

THE BIG LIE:
BIRTHERS AND TRUTHERS

Somewhere beyond right and left lies the *fright* wing of American politics: a place of paranoia where diabolical plots are hatched by opponents in power and only true patriots with special knowledge of these conspiracies have the courage to ask the tough questions.

The Big Lie can be seductive. It masquerades as reason, but it leads down a path confirming your worst fears about your worst enemy. In the first decade of the twenty-first century there have been two Big Lies that that have preoccupied the fright wingers—the ideas that Barack Obama was not born in America (the Birthers) and that 9/11 was an inside job (the Truthers). On the surface they seem like opposite sides of the same coin—an anti-Obama conspiracy theory for Wingnuts on the right and an anti-Bush conspiracy theory for Wingnuts on the left. But nothing is that simple among the fright wing. As I dug around this dark, dank basement, I discovered that the Birther claims were first circulated by Obama's opponents on the far left during the 2008 primary campaign. And the Truther myths are now most aggressively promoted by anti-government activists on the far right.

Both conspiracy theories aim at the foundation of the respective president's claim to history—Obama's importance as the first African-American president and Bush's leadership after 9/11. Both claims try to undermine the presidents' essential legitimacy by writing an alternate history, one that would reveal them to be monstrous frauds with dictatorial ambitions. Proponents of the Big Lie cast themselves as populist truth tellers taking on powerful interests, but their ultimate goal is to bring down their political opponents while proving that the American people are easily duped, making their own efforts seem both misunderstood and heroic.

While some Wingnut claims take place in political theory, like casting Obama as a communist, the Big Lie often poses as scientific inquiry. Countless hours have been wasted pouring through data, learning alternate histories and ignoring the obvious while trying to get to the truth behind the Big Lie. The obsessions of the more extreme Wingnuts are impermeable to reason. Back in the eighteenth century, the author of *Gulliver's Travels,* Irish satirist Jonathan Swift, identified why: "You cannot reason someone out of something he has not been reasoned into."

Those on the periphery have always peddled the Big Lie. What's different now? As the fringe blurs with the base, and the Internet provides an effective platform, more people in American politics are beginning to buy into it.

The Birthers

"I don't want this flag to change! I want my country back!" screams the lady in red at Republican Congressman Mike Castle's Delaware Town Hall.

With brown hair pulled back and wearing an oversized red T-shirt, she's waving her birth certificate and a tiny American flag in her left hand with a microphone in the right. "I want to go back to January 20. Why are you people ignoring his birth certificate? He is not an American citizen!" Her voice rises an octave and cracks with anger. "He is a citizen of Kenya!"

The crowd goes nuts with screams of support. The woman known to locals as "Crazy Eileen" has brought a small army, and they have the place packed.

Mike Castle seems taken aback. After a bit of circuitous stammering, he says, "If you're referring to the president, he is a citizen of the United States." He is shouted down in tones that recall the crowd in *Monty Python and the Holy Grail* yelling, "Burn the witch!" Castle continues, "You can boo, but he *is* a citizen of the United States." Crazy Eileen then led the crowd in rowdy rendition of the Pledge of Allegiance.

A video of the confrontation soon went viral and America was introduced to the "Birthers"—conspiracy theorists committed to undoing the 2008 presidential election by trying to prove that Barack Obama was not born in the United States.

To them, this president is not just anti-American but constitutionally ineligible for office. It's the ultimate fright-wing paranoid fantasy—we have a Muslim illegal alien in the White House.

It's all part of a carefully constructed plot: "The Muslims have said they plan on destroying the U.S. from the inside out. What better way to start than at the highest level, through the President of the United States, one of their own!"[2] Or so said an e-mail chain during the 2008 campaign. At the same time, Internet rumors were making the case that Obama was born not in the United States but in Kenya—his Muslim father's home country. The ideas got linked: A poll in Tennessee found that one-third of respondents thought that Obama was either "definitely" or "probably" a Muslim or born outside the United States.[3]

But these Manchurian candidate myths seemed too ridiculous to mention in mainstream media until the Birther Town Hall video clip revolt crystallized a subterranean effort to raise the issue, reaching talk radio, cable news, the armed services and even the halls of Congress.

The rumor has its roots in the original Obama Haters, the PUMAs—Party Unity My Ass. It was a splinter group of hard-core Hillary Clinton supporters who did not want to give up the ghost after the bitter fifty-state Bataan Death March to the Democratic nomination.

In the early summer of 2008, message boards on sites like PUMAParty.com began indulging in the ultimate reversal-of-fortune fantasy—that the party nomination could be overturned on constitutional grounds. "Obama May Be Illegal To Be Elected President!" read one e-mail: "This came from a USNA [U.S. Naval Academy] alumnus. It'll be interesting to see how the media handle this. . . . WRITE TO YOUR LOCAL newspaper editors etc. Keep this out there everyday possible. Also write to the DNC too!"[4]

In June, the Obama campaign released his birth certificate on its Web site as part of its "fight the smears" effort. Factcheck.org and other organizations examined the document in person and declared it genuine: "Our conclusion: Obama was born in the U.S.A. just as he has always said."[5] But posters at the PUMA sites were unimpressed: "Nobody believes it's for real, except the Kool-Aid drinkers themselves."[6]

A Hillary supporter from Texas, Linda Starr, was particularly fired up by what she called "the daily misogynistic hate speech against Hillary" during the primaries. As a Democratic precinct captain in Medina County, she had volunteered for the Clinton campaign during the hotly contested June Lone Star state primary and been a Hillary delegate at the state convention. But Linda's real talent was as an amateur opposition researcher—she'd dug up information against Republican congressional leaders like Dan Burton and Bob Livingston during the Clinton impeachment hearings of the late 1990s and was cited as a key source for CBS's discredited 2004 investigation into George W. Bush's National Guard records that led to Dan Rather's replacement after twenty-four years as the evening news anchor.[7] After Hillary's concession, Linda Starr turned her attention to Barack Obama. "I determined that I was going to start digging up every bit of dirt that I could find on him," she told me, "and that hopefully that I would find something against him that would convince the Democratic Party to dump him and make Hillary the nominee."[8]

In the first week of August, as the Democrats were getting ready for their convention in Denver, Philadelphia attorney Philip Berg got a call from Linda offering a challenge. "She called me up and said, 'Have you heard about Obama not being national born?' I said, 'Yes.' She said, 'Well, now it's for real, and you're the only attorney in the country with brass balls enough to sue Obama.'"[9]

Berg is a Democrat and he'd also been a Hillary supporter. But he was best known as a former deputy attorney general of Pennsylvania and a serial unsuccessful campaigner for statewide office with a reputation as an enthusiastic litigant. In 2004, he filed a 9/11 Truther lawsuit against President Bush alleging that the government allowed 9/11 to happen and that the World Trade Center was destroyed from within.[10] Now he had a new conspiracy to push.

On August 21, Berg filed the first Birther lawsuit, asking for an injunction to stop the convention from going forward, alleging that Obama was born in Kenya, not Hawaii. He faxed notices to the DNC (Democratic National Committee) and Obama campaign headquarters.

He launched the Web site Obamacrimes.com the next day with Linda's assistance. The lawsuit went nowhere. Berg told me: "[DNC chair] Howard Dean at that point should have called Obama and said 'What's the story, are you natural born or not?' . . . Obviously there was collusion there and I think when it's all said and done they should all be tried and put in jail." The media ignored it as well. "I wish I could sue them," says Berg, of the media. "If the American public knew what was going on here Obama would be out of office or we never would have had him in office."

In July 2009, soon after Crazy Eileen's shout-down of Mike Castle went viral, a U.S. army major, Stefan Frederick Cook, brought the Birther story its first national headlines when he refused deployment to Afghanistan on the grounds that President Barack Obama might not be a natural-born citizen and therefore would be constitutionally ineligible to give orders as commander in chief. Major Cook, a distinguished combat veteran, appears to have been a willing pawn in the Birthers' efforts to bring attention to their cause. He had volunteered for Afghan deployment in May, with the intention of carrying out the political performance-art litigation.

The military shrugged and said since he volunteered to go to AfPak he was within his rights to change his mind. No lawsuit was needed. An e-mail or a phone call would have been fine. But they issued a statement just to be clear: "This in no way validates any of the outlandish claims made by Major Cook," and a judge threw out the case. Unfazed, the Birthers celebrated it as a smoking-gun victory.

WorldNetDaily trumpeted the news as "Bombshell: Orders Revoked for Soldier Challenging Prez." Cook's lawyer, an Orange County dentist with an on-line legal degree named Orly Taitz, subsequently announced there were 170 more soldiers willing to file similar protests against the president. The blond middle-aged mother of three was on a mission.

Taitz first stumbled across the controversy while surfing the Internet. As a native of the former Soviet Republic of Moldova, she sniffed a communist conspiracy. Or maybe it was Nazi. "I realized that Obama was another Stalin," she said. "It's a cross between Stalinist USSR and Nazi Germany."[11] On October 25, 2008, two weeks before the election, she e-mailed the California secretary of state's office, asking about the "eligibility of Barack Hussein Obama." On the field inquiring how she became aware of this problem, Taitz typed "native intelligence."

She may be crazy, but she's not stupid. Taitz became the face of the Birther lawsuits in the media, making twenty-nine trips across the United States in 2009, filing more lawsuits and doing more than 100 interviews. WordNetDaily profiled her generously: "Meet Fierce Blonde Behind Obama Eligibility Lawsuits."[12] And she's got the snappy name-calling sound bite down: "Obama should be in the Big House, not the White House!"[13] On her blog, the tone gets a wee bit more unhinged, repeatedly calling the Obama administration the "Gestapo-SS establishment," extending the metaphor with a call for investigation and execution: "They all should and would be tried in Nurenberg (sic) style trials for harassing, intimidating, blackmailing and terrorizing fellow citizens, for defrauding the whole country."[14]

Fox News's Sean Hannity picked up the torch, and so did another mainstream heavyweight Lou Dobbs, who had her on his radio show and segued into a CNN segment on the Cook case by saying, "New questions are being raised about Obama's eligibility to serve as president."[15] Dobbs, whom Taitz refers to as a "supporter," has since resigned from the network and appears to be contemplating a political career.

With her 15 minutes of fame ticking, Taitz appeared on CNN alongside co-litigant Alan Keyes to debate the issue. I was tapped to take them on alongside my friend Errol Louis, a columnist for the *New York Daily News*. Taitz and Keyes were beaming in remotely via satellite, but I got to watch their pre-game rituals: Keyes had his eyes closed as if in prayer; Taitz was jumpy and pie-eyed.

Anchor Kitty Pilgrim went through a semi-exasperated three-and-a-half-minute dismantling of the Birther arguments, including the long-ago issuance of Obama's August 1961 certificate of live birth, its validation by Hawaii's Republican governor, Linda Lingle, and two birth announcements published in Honolulu papers.

Asked what more he needed to be convinced, Keyes's response was an instant classic in the clueless overconfidence of conspiracy theorists: "Some evidence."

My on-air summation was also four syllables: "You guys are nuts."

The eleven Republican members of Congress who co-sponsored the so-called Birther bill apparently disagree. In response to the hysteria, H.R 1503 would require presidential campaigns to provide "a copy of the candidate's birth certificate." When asked whether Obama "is a U.S. citizen," bill co-sponsor Randy Neugebauer (R-TX) gave a Texas two-step reply: "I don't know. I've never seen him produce documents that would say one way or another."[16]

But in a refreshing break from the "no enemies on the right" straightjacket, some conservatives knew that things were getting indefensibly overheated. Michael Medved memorably denounced the Birthers as "crazy, nutburger, demagogue, money-hungry, exploitative, irresponsible, filthy conservative imposters" who are "the worst enemy of the conservative movement" and "make us look sick, troubled and not suitable for civilized company."[17]

With the Birther controversy ingrained in the Wingnut history of the first year of Obama, I flew to California to reacquaint myself with birther queen Orly Taitz, this time face-to-face.

Nestled in the hills of Rancho Santa Margarita, Taitz's law office and dental practice stand in a Spanish mission—style office park. In their cluttered corridors, she balances the demands of a small private practice with an effort to prove that the president of the United States is constitutionally ineligible for office.

Taitz greets me at the door wearing a bright purple and orange dress. She seems engaging and friendly to her employees, concerned about her clients and highly organized. Details of the full conspiracy are copied and filed inside black binders with colored tabs.

On the walls of her office are pictures of her three sons wearing their Tae Kwon Do uniforms from years past. When asked to describe herself, she says, "I am a proud mother of three sons and a wife and a professional woman who's been working all her life." In any other context, she would be a classic American immigrant success story, but over the span of one year she has placed herself at the forefront of a massive conspiracy theory.

"I'm just concerned that our constitutional freedoms are being taken away," she explains. She's established the Defense of Freedom foundation and blogs on her Web site.[17] She talks about the hundreds of e-mails she gets from supporters who want to help with her work, and the death threats that are coming in daily. To show her depth of secret support, she says Sarah Palin has friended her on Facebook, along with Newt Gingrich, RNC Chairman Michael Steele, House Minority Whip Eric Cantor and Israeli Prime Minister Benjamin Netanyahu. Then it's time to get down to business.

The conspiracy goes deep, and so does the paperwork. She hands me a fifty-page packet that she says is a

copy of what she has sent to Attorney General Eric
Holder. It is a hodgepodge of letters and legal documents, Web site homepages and data lists.

Taitz shows me Obama's official certificate of live
birth and contrasts it with the long-form certificate. She
presents an oft-touted piece of Hawaiian legislation, Act
182, which makes it possible for children born out of
state to receive birth certificates, but the bill itself indicates that it didn't take effect until 1983.

She's got two copies of Obama's alleged Kenyan birth
certificate, which she says were sent to her anonymously. "So I had both the registrar copy and a hospital
copy from Kenya but yet there wasn't one proper birth
certificate from the United States."

Then she hands over the mother lode, her newest project: "I have put together a database showing he used
thirty-nine different Social Security numbers. . . . This is
a felony. For those kind of criminal activities, for those
kind of felonies, people spend years and years in prison.
And when you multiply this by thirty-nine, we're talking
a life sentence." She shows me a new affidavit from an
Ohio private investigator swearing that Barack Obama's
social security number—which she gives me digit for
digit—was issued in the state of Connecticut in the mid-
1970s but actually belonged to a man born in 1890.

"This is mind-boggling that we have the president
and commander in chief of all U.S. military who is using
a stolen Social Security number. I did investigation to
find out where he got it and what I found out was that

his grandmother, Madeline, volunteered in Oahu Circuit Court in Probate Department. Now, Probate Department is the department where you get the Social Security numbers." That's right. Obama's grandma stole him a social security number back in the '70s.

When you've got that many different ways to say that someone is an evil psychotic fraud, it's possible there is some projection going on. And then there's her legal record to date—a perfect .000 batting average. Phil Berg had warned me about Taitz in paranoid hall of mirror terms, saying, "I really think she's a plant. I think she's been put there to disrupt everything to make us look like fools." But could an otherwise intelligent, sincere and accomplished woman be so single-issue insane, like the political equivalent of a functioning alcoholic?

When I got to the Long Beach airport I began paging through the full fifty-page packet full of documents and screen shots that she gave me. I started to read her open letter to Attorney General Holder, which was cc'd to fifty state governors and the entire U.S. Senate. It demanded "investigation and immediate action" into fourteen counts of "criminal activity/crimes," among them: cyberspace crimes, impersonation of a military officer, libel, defamation of character, intimidation, harassment, interference with judicial proceedings, breaking into the computer system of the Supreme Court, voter fraud and forgery.

It is a long, rambling letter, and life is short, but early on she sets out her demands and identifies the

consequences: ". . . Verify the above facts brought forward by me and demand Obama/Soetoro's immediate
resignation or removal from office due to fraud and Constitutional inability. National security and national survival depends on your expedient actions as Obama/
Soetoro releases violent terrorists from Gitmo, allocates
$900 million to Gaza ruled by radical Hamas terrorists,
signs an executive order that would provide expedient
U.S. citizenship and bring hundreds of thousands of
Hamas terrorists to this country."

Then she details an alleged pattern of harassment:
"When around the same time one gets her case erased
from the docket of the Supreme Court and Wikipedia, a
tire blows out on her in a car, and a link with a sign in
Arabic about somebody's hanging appears, one begins
to feel threatened. I believe all the occurrences had to do
with my investigation, not only in the area of Obama/
Soetoro's ineligibility for the presidency, but also in the
financial dealings of Barack and Michelle Obama."

And finally, she offers a bargain to the feds: "As a private citizen I cannot complete this investigation. However, you, as Attorney General, together with the FBI,
IRS, Secret Service and local law enforcement can and
have an obligation to complete it. I would be willing to
complete this investigation if you're willing to grant me
a status of relater-special prosecutor. Sincerely, Dr. Orly
Taitz, Esquire"

As I finished, I was reminded of U.S. District Judge
Clay D. Land's comments to Taitz when he dismissed

one of her Birther complaints: "Unlike in *Alice in Wonderland,* simply saying something is so does not make it so."[18]

By then the Birther case had been heard about by millions of Americans—and a July 2009 poll found that 58 percent of Republicans either thought Barack Obama wasn't born in the United States or weren't sure.[19]

The 9/11 Truthers

Somewhere in the world of Wingnut conspiracy theories, left and right overlap. And when you can rally around both Texan libertarian Ron Paul and Georgia leftist Cynthia McKinney as presidential nominees, you've hit a very special place of trans-partisan paranoia.

Welcome to the world of the 9/11 Truthers.

The attacks of September 11, 2001, were the most digitally documented loss of human life in history, exploding on our television screens in real time. And yet, an Internet-driven conspiracy theory soon set in—fueled by Bush Derangement Syndrome—arguing that the U.S. government, and not al-Qaeda, was behind the attack. To quote from one online screed, "The actual forces behind the conception, planning, and execution of this seminal event came not from bearded Islamic extremists living in a cave in Afghanistan, but from within high-level rogue elements of our own government."

This could be dismissed as somewhere between offensive and absurd, if it weren't for the fact that in the years since the attacks, the conspiracy theory's credibility has been on the rise.

Five years after the attack, a Scripps poll found 36 percent of Americans believed the federal government "either assisted in the 9/11 attacks or took no action" because they "wanted to go to war in the Middle East." Sixteen percent thought the World Trade Center might have collapsed because of secret explosives, while 12 percent said a U.S. cruise missile—and not a hijacked airplane—hit the Pentagon.[20]

In the Bush era, liberal congressmen and celebrities were eager to get on the bandwagon.

Then-Congresswoman Cynthia McKinney reflexively reached for Watergate rhetoric, asking, "What did this administration know and when did it know it, about the events of September 11?"[21] Congressman Dennis Kucinich rallied the crowd at a Code Pink protest by saying, "We have a plan, Mr. President, and our plan is to tell the truth about 9/11."[22] Michael Moore told a group of 9/11 Truthers he had questions about the plane that hit the Pentagon. "Why don't they want us to see that plane coming into the building? . . . I don't think the official investigations have told us the complete truth. They haven't even told us half the truth."[23] Rosie O'Donnell weighed in by saying, "It is impossible for a building to fall the way it fell without explosives being involved." And signatories of the 9/11 Truth petition included Ralph Nader, Janeane Garofalo, Howard Zinn, Edward Asner and President Obama's onetime Green Jobs czar Van Jones.

Sadly and stupidly, they were not alone. Type "9/11 Conspiracy" into Google and you'll get millions of page matches—8,730,000 on November 29, 2009. The site 9/11truth.org includes a site, Lawyers for 9/11 Truth, which presents a score of endorsements by "legal scholars, judges and attorneys" for the statement: "We are demanding an end to the 9/11 cover-up, and a full investigation by unbiased people with subpoena power . . . and the courage to demand that the Constitution and rule of law are followed, and all guilty persons held accountable for their actions."

Purple bumper stickers reading "9/11 was an Inside Job" became as annoyingly common in the '00s as "Andre the Giant Has a Posse" stickers were in the '90s. And in the summer of 2008, New Yorkers were stopped on street corners by petitioners seeking signatures for the creation of "a new, independent investigation of the attacks" that will "follow the evidence wherever it might lead."

Like many New Yorkers, I lived through the attacks and their aftermath. I saw the first plane scream past my window and was covered in ash after the collapse. I was there. Afterwards, I spent three months writing eulogies for the fallen firefighters and police officers as a speechwriter for Mayor Rudy Giuliani. So when I see people in Lower Manhattan indulging the Blame-America-First reflex, I lose my sense of humor.

In search of some perspective, I called Professor Patrick J. Leman, a conspiracy theory specialist at the

University of London, to ask a decidedly un-academic question: *What the hell is going on?*

"There is an underlying psychological phenomena called 'major-event/major-cause' thinking," explained Dr. Leman. "If there's a big event, we like to find a similarly big cause to explain what happened. It provides us with a sense that the world is a relatively predictable place. Because the alternative—imagining that something big, like the death of a president, can be caused by something minor like a lone gunman—presents us with a view of the world that's unpredictable and scary and difficult to control."

The greatest check against government conspiracy is the up-close chaos of any human organization. People are simply too disorganized and indiscreet to pull off a secret world-wide plot. But it turns out that the Orwellian-named 9/11 Truthers need a Big Brother for their story to hold.

"Conspiracy theorists need a competent and malevolent conspirator," said Dr. Leman. "And if you have a lot of Keystone Kops messing around, that's not going to work very well. So there is a kind of contradiction here: 'They're up to no good, but they're very good at it.'"

This requires that 9/11 Truthers effectively reverse-engineer a well-documented al-Qaeda plot to bring down the Twin Towers. They would rather believe that their own government is all-powerful and evil than imperfect and well-intentioned. Faced with a real conspiracy they must invent their own.

Investigating the 9/11 conspiracy Web sites is a
thankless business—as the old saying goes, When you
argue with a fool, you've got two fools. They drape their
paranoia in the American flag and earnest prose. The
catalogue of accusations is dizzying—a Top 40 list is
available on 911truth.org—but the usual suspects include explosives to bring down the Twin Towers, missiles to hit the Pentagon, Dick Cheney complicit, the
military and the FAA gone MIA. The documentary
Loose Change—an X-Files–tempoed account of the conspiracy by upstate New York twenty-somethings—has
been viewed on You Tube more than 3 million times.

Alternately, you can just take Osama bin Laden's
word for it. He's repeatedly taken credit for the attacks,
including on a videotape where he recounts the planning process and his wish for maximum damage: "We
calculated in advance the number of casualties from the
enemy, who would be killed based on the position of the
tower. We calculated that the floors that would be hit
would be three or four floors. I was the most optimistic
of them all. . . . Due to my experience in this field, I was
thinking that the fire from the gas in the plane would
melt the iron structure of the building and collapse the
area where the plane hit and all the floors above it only.
This is all that we hoped for."[24]

But this tape is dismissed by the Truthers: "The man
shown in the video, though bearded, Arabic, and of
darkish complexion, is much heavier than bin Laden.
The man in the video is seen writing something down

with his right hand. Bin Laden is well-known to be left-handed." Similarly dismissed are the voluminous *9/11 Commission Report* and the thorough special report by *Popular Mechanics, Debunking the 9/11 Myths*. As Dr. Leman says, "A conspiracy theorist is always going to see a conspiracy—whatever evidence you give to them."

The conspiracy theories continued to be pumped up even after the Bush administration ended, promoted by fright-wing anti-government radio hosts like Alex Jones and disturbingly mainstream liberal celebrity dupes like Charlie Sheen, who demanded and was denied a request to brief President Obama on the matter.[25] Thanks, Charlie.

The dogged search for truth is admirable and essential to a free society. But when that concept becomes twisted by a moral relativism that masquerades as open inquiry, the idea of truth starts to lose its meaning. Ignoring the obvious does not lead to insight. And by entertaining conspiracy theories after being attacked, we run the risk of amusing ourselves to death.

Just because an evil ideology expresses its murderous intentions with cartoonish clarity doesn't mean that they are not deadly serious. We have the body count to prove otherwise. So let's call the 9/11 Truthers what they are—al-Qaeda apologists.

THE HATRIOTS:
ARMED AND DANGEROUS

The plan to assassinate the president was called Operation Patriot. Marine Lance Corporal Kody Brittingham plotted from his barracks at Camp LeJeune, North Carolina. With maps of the Capitol Building and a dossier on Barack Obama, he penned a letter explaining his reasons for wanting to join the ranks of John Wilkes Booth and Lee Harvey Oswald:

> I Kody Brittingham, write this as a letter of intent. I am in full mental health and clear judgment, having consciously made a decision, and in turn do so choose to carry out the actions entailed. I have sworn to defend my country, my constitution, and the values and virtues of the aforementioned. My vow was to protect against all enemies, both foreign and domestic. I have found, through much research, evidence to support my current state of mind. Having found said domestic enemy, it is my duty and honor to carry out by all means necessary to protect my nation and her people from this threat.[1]

Kody Brittingham was arrested before his plot had a chance to be enacted. President Obama spoke at Camp

LeJeune in February 2009 without incident, announcing his plan to draw down U.S. forces from Iraq. But Brittingham's clear, cold-blooded rationalization for assassination—a patriot defending the Constitution against the president by any means necessary—reflected the rhetoric of the emerging Hatriot movement.

They are self-styled patriots armed and ready for a new American Revolution. They talk of martial law, a seizure of guns and imposition of global government, complete with forced internment camps and mass executions. When love of country is mixed with fear of the government and hate for the president, that's when you become a Hatriot.

"You need to be alert and aware of how close we are to having our constitutional republic destroyed!"

So thundered Stewart Rhodes to a wave of applause on Lexington Green, Massachusetts, on April 19, 2009. The crowd assembled including military veterans and reservists, cops and firefighters, and no small number of Revolutionary War re-enactors. It was the first public meeting of the Oath Keepers. The location and date of the gathering had been chosen carefully. It was the anniversary of the first battle of the American Revolution on that very spot. The Oath Keeper Web site featured a quote from George Washington to set the tone: "The time is now near at hand which must probably determine, whether Americans are to be, Freemen, or Slaves; whether they are to have any property they can call their own." The Oath Keepers then added their own dark warning: "Such a time is near at hand again."[2]

But April 19th has deeper significance for members of the militia movement and their inheritors throughout the United States. It is the date that federal officers attacked the Branch Davidian compound in Waco, Texas. And it's the day that Timothy McVeigh blew up the Murrah Federal Building in Oklahoma City, killing 168 people. McVeigh was wearing a T-shirt that day with a favorite Hatriot message handed down from Thomas Jefferson: "The Tree of Liberty must be refreshed from time to time with the blood of patriots and tyrants."

Within nine months of their first meeting, Oath Keeper dues-paying membership rose to 3,000—including active-duty military, current and retired police officers and sheriffs—and the organization claims that 15,000 people have signed up to participate on their online forum. They have established themselves as a nonprofit organization, complete with a board of directors. Describing themselves as "The Guardians of the Republic," the Oath Keepers distribute business cards with orders they will not obey—it's a step-by-step tour through the Hatriot vision of America. Among them:

- We will NOT obey any order to disarm the American people.
- We will NOT obey orders to invade and subjugate any state that asserts its sovereignty and declares

the national government to be in violation of the compact by which that state entered the Union.

- We will NOT obey any order to blockade American cities, thus turning them into giant concentration camps.
- We will NOT obey any order to force American citizens into any form of detention camps under any pretext.
- We will NOT obey orders to assist or support the use of any foreign troops on U.S. soil against the American people to "keep the peace" or to "maintain control" during any emergency, or under any other pretext. We will consider such use of foreign troops against our people to be an invasion and an act of war.

It's a world of government-sponsored concentration camps, forced disarmament and international invasion—scary stuff. But where many see fearmongering, the Oath Keepers see themselves as freedom's last defender. Stewart Rhodes is an engaging and intelligent if angry, guy—he's taken the stage on MSNBC's *Hardball* and won a constitutional prize at Yale Law. He is careful to distance his group from outright advocates of anti-government violence, writing that "those of you who are in militia have a vital mission which we support and agree with fully. But it is a different mission. We don't mind at all if people belong to both, but keep the two activities separate." He also knows the way to disarm critics: To those who see the rise of the Oath Keepers as a response to Obama, he is quick to condemn George W. Bush—he was just too busy during the Bush years to mobilize his ideas into action. And to those who question the repeated concentration camp riff, he pulls the ultimate liberal guilt trip: If internment camps happened to Japanese-Americans during World War II, why should we think it couldn't happen today. It raises the image of Stewart Rhodes, liberal action hero.

But not all Oath Keepers are as smooth as Stewart Rhodes. In a video posted on the Oath Keepers' site, a man who describes himself as a former army paratrooper in Afghanistan and Iraq calls President Obama "an enemy of the state," adding, "I would rather die than be a slave to my government." Oath Keeper and former Arizona Sheriff Richard Mack has said, "The greatest threat we face today is not terrorists; it is our federal government."[3] Extremism is no vice in Hatriot circles: you can even buy T-shirts at the Oath Keeper site that say: "I'm a Right Wing Extremist and Damn Proud of It!"

The Hatriot movement has morphed from the militia movements of the mid-1990s. The Southern Poverty Law Center estimates that more than 125 new hate groups and 350 new Nativist groups have sprung up since 2005.[4] "One big difference from the militia movement of the 1990s," the SPLC points out, "is that the face of the federal government—the enemy that almost all parts of the extreme right see as the primary threat to freedom—is now black."[5]

The Three Percenters are another new breed of Hatriot, who, like the Oath Keepers, focus on armed resistance and American Revolutionary War imagery. They take their name from the questionable statistic that only 3 percent of the American colonists actively fought for independence. Therefore the Three Percenters are not only an elite group but also a direct link to the Founding Fathers, making their extremist alienation from mainstream America a badge of honor and secret knowledge. They describe themselves, as "promoting the ideals of liberty, freedom and a constitutional government restrained by law."[6] But beneath the benign bumper sticker, the loosely affiliated group also professes that they "embrace the American Resistance Movement philosophy"—a survivalist militia-incubating network that teaches its followers how to train for the coming fight against tyranny. Their online forums offer a glimpse into a lunatic fringe that is itching to get the fight on: "This government has failed," writes one registered user known as JV67. "At what point do we follow the example of the Founding Fathers and take up arms against these tyrants?"[7]

Three Percenter founder, Mike Vanderboegh, of Pinson, Alabama, is a self-described "former leftist" and SDS member who had a political epiphany reading Nobel economist Friedrich von Hayek's *The Road to Serfdom* in the mid-1970s. He became a Second Amendment activist and was involved in the militia movement during the 1990s. The father of three now reluctantly believes the escalation is all but inevitable. As he chronicles the first year of the Obama administration, particularly the attempts to pass health-care legislation, he is bracing for revolution: "You should understand that we are rapidly coming to a point in this country when half of the people are going to become convinced of the illegitimacy of this administration and its designs upon our liberty. Need I remind you that this side is the one with most of the firearms?"[8]

Now Vanderboegh is warning his supporters to be prepared for "The Big Die Off": "When a computer crashes, you simply discard it and obtain another. When political systems, nations or civilizations fail, they collapse in a welter of blood and carnage, usually ending in mountains of bodies, slavery and a long dark night of tyranny. This is referred to by people today who recognize the existential danger by the short-hand acronym of 'TBDO'—'The Big Die Off.' This is not a video game. There are no do-overs. This is as real as it gets. Your system has experienced one or more fatal errors and must shut down at this time. Whether you survive The Big Die Off with anything left that is worth preserving is up to you."[9] As Vanderboegh's home page warns, "All politics in this country now is just dress rehearsal for civil war."

The Far Right Flirts with Secession

After speaking at an Austin Tea Party rally where the crowd repeatedly shouted, "Secede!", Republican Governor Rick Perry was asked about renewed talk of Texas secession: "There's a lot of different scenarios," he said. "We've got a great union. There's absolutely no reason to dissolve it. But if Washington continues to thumb their nose at the American people, you know, who knows what might come out of that? Texas is a very unique place. . . . when we came to the Union in 1845, one of the issues was that we would be able to leave if we decided to do that."[10]

The folks from Fox News were carrying the Texas Tea Party live and couldn't help but weigh in on Perry's comments.

GRETA VAN SUSTEREN: You know, from here, Glenn, listening to Governor Perry last night and watching your crowd and listening to the things that are coming out of Texas—I don't want to be too dramatic, but it almost seems like Texas is going to secede from the rest of the nation.

GLENN BECK: I mean, I don't know—can we get this back here? [Points to a banner] This is on the jib back over here. This says "Texas independence" . . . And the reason is—correct me if I'm wrong—these people love America. They just think Texas does America best![11]

Suddenly, somehow, the threat of secession is a sign of super-patriotism.

Just days before, Beck had been musing on-air about the same subject: "Does the individual have any rights anymore? Does the state have any rights anymore? And I know, because I've heard it, from all of the conservative historians and scholars, and everything else. But you can't convince me that the founding fathers wouldn't allow you to secede. The Constitution is not a suicide pact. And if a state says, I don't want to go there, because that's suicide, they have a right to back out. They have a right. People have a right to not commit economic suicide. . . . I sign into this Union, and I can never get out, no matter what the government does? I can never get out? Well that leaves only one other option. That doesn't seem like a good option."[12]

You'd think the Civil War had cleared up any questions about the efficacy of the "other option" Beck is talking about—600,000 Americans died. But conservative activists keep circling back to the concept, something that would have presumably given them offense if it had been suggested one year before during the presidency of Texan George W. Bush.

Here's Academy Award–winning actor Jon Voight playing his newfound political role as a conservative pundit in an August interview with the *Washington Times*: "There's a real question at stake now. Is President Obama creating a civil war in our own country?"[13]

Focus on the Family's James Dobson offered a similar applause line at the Council for National Policy: "We are in greater danger right now I think than at any time since the Civil War. . . . What this country desperately needs in coming elections are . . . men and women who cherish liberty and are willing to give their very lives for it and will oppose the evil of liberalism."[14]

The impulse occasionally gets dressed up as intellec-
tualism, with a summer 2009 column in the *American
Thinker* foreseeing "several regional republics" taking
the place of the United States after a civil war inspired
by the "overbearing, oppressive leviathan" created by
Barack Obama.[15]

In anticipation of a civil war, the Oath Keepers include state sovereignty among its list of orders they
will not obey: "In response to the obscene growth of
federal power and to the absurdly totalitarian claimed
powers of the Executive. . . . We will NOT obey orders
to invade and subjugate any state that asserts its sovereignty and declares the national government to be in
violation of the compact by which that state entered
the Union."

And a new Idaho militia was established in 2009 by
army veteran James Ambrose, who explained his decision along the same lines: "I formed it to defend Idaho if
it wants to secede. If Idaho decides it no longer wants to
be part of the United States, we back that decision."[16]

So perhaps it wasn't a surprise that when the Senate
Health Care Bill was presented in October 2009, the
Wingnut netroots were quick to pick up the civil war
talk in postings on sites like Michelle Malkin's HotAir:

- "I don't want to suggest violence, but I think this
  nation is headed towards a civil war if things don't
  stop. The American people can't take a whole lot
  more of this."[17]

- "Maybe it is time the non Marxist states considered 'opting out' of the 'union.'"
- "I'd sooner die a patriot, than a slave. And even if every one of us is killed . . . I will have considered it an honor to be dead amongst other like minded heroes. Secession and civil war are alternatives to this, and by god if those are the only options left . . . so be it, the democrats forced our hand)"[18]

Overheated echo-chamber chatter about secession and civil war might seem simply creepy if eight states hadn't recently passed secession resolutions.

On April Fool's Day 2009, the conservative Georgia State Senate passed a resolution by a vote of forty-three to one threatening to secede from the United States. It was a fool's resolution, but it was not a joke.

It was the work of the Tenthers—advocates of reaffirming the Tenth Amendment. Under the innocuous-sounding banner of "Affirming states' rights based on Jeffersonian principles,"[19] the resolution resuscitated Confederate and segregation-era arguments about nullification—the right of states to nullify the Constitution and disband the United States if the president or federal government assumes powers not explicitly provided for.

The resolution had been co-sponsored by some of the most senior members of the state legislature, including the senate majority leader and president pro-tem. Among the areas enumerated in the Georgia resolution were "Further infringements on the right to keep and bear arms including prohibitions of type or quantity of arms or ammunition"—in other words, a reinstatement of the federal assault weapons ban could trigger Georgia to secede from the union. It also reserved to Georgia the right to judge "how far the licentiousness of speech and of the press may be abridged without lessening their useful freedom." The Taliban might have approved.

The strangeness of the Tenthers was put into context by *Atlanta Journal-Constitution* columnist Jay Bookman: "The resolution they sponsored is part of a radical right-wing national movement. . . . And while the Georgia resolution is legally meaningless and was passed without debate or even knowledge of most senators, it has had an impact. It has been hailed by, among others, those fighting the conspiracy to create a single North American country, by the Confederate States Militia, by the John Birch Society, and the League of the South, which still pines for the cause of an 'independent South' and believes that 'Southern society is radically different from the society impressed upon it by an alien occupier.'"[20]

In its commitment to conservative secession, the League of the South not only echoes the usual Wingnut talking points about "national socialism: coming to a town near you" but offers books connecting Lincoln to Marx and Hitler as a "Band of Brothers."[21] It's the same grouping President Obama is often placed alongside at the Tea Party rallies. Other strains of the neo-Confederate movement find themselves a home in the Hatriot movement, advancing the pseudo-Constitutionalist idea of

"Fourteenth Amendment Citizens"—aka African-Americans—who, because their rights were granted by the U.S. government after the Civil War, do not fall under natural law as described by the Declaration of Independence and are therefore lesser citizens than natural-born whites. It's an arcane example of the lengths to which white supremacists will go to defend bigotry as being sanctioned by the Bible or the Founding Fathers. But I digress.

The *Gone with the Wind* state wasn't the only one to sign up for the Tenth Amendment insanity. Similar resolutions passed in Oklahoma, North Dakota, South Dakota, Tennessee, Idaho, Louisiana and Alaska—all states won by McCain-Palin in 2008. And Sarah Palin, whose husband was a member of the secessionist Alaska Independence Party for ten years, was one of the few governors to put her signature on the bill, before resigning in the summer of 2009.

Populist conservative appeals, anti–federal government impulses and threats of secession are nothing new, but they take on special resonance with a black president in a bad economy.

Hatriot History, Media and Murder

America has seen militarized right-wing radical groups in the past, playing off the same fears: a tyrannical federal government, a surrender of sovereignty and seizure of all guns.

Survivalist groups like the Minutemen began developing a "patriotic resistance" movement patterned after
colonial militias in the early 1960s, doing wilderness
military drills, hoarding weapons and ammunition to
prepare for a Soviet invasion in advance of what they
said was a plan to "confiscate all private fire-arms by
the end of 1965."[22] Its founder, Robert Bolivar DePugh,
briefly tried to form a political party, dubbed the Patriot
Party, but his plans for political influence were undone
when he was arrested for a plot to blow up the Red-
mond, Washington, City Hall and surrounding power
plants, before robbing local banks.[23] Arrests of affiliated
Minutemen groups found half-baked plans for a cyanide
attack on the United Nations[24] and extensive weapons
caches including bombs, mortars, machine guns and
more than one million rounds of ammunition.[25]

Major General Edwin Walker became a hero to mid-
century right-wing militants when he resigned from the
military after coming under criticism for distributing
John Birch Society literature to troops. The decorated
World War II and Korean War combat veteran then led
protests against James Meredith's integration of the University of Mississippi. His rallying cry presaged Wingnut and Hatriot claims today, calling for "a national
protest against the conspiracy from within. Rally to the
cause of freedom in righteous indignation, violent vocal
protest, and bitter silence under the flag of Mississippi
at the use of Federal troops . . . This is the conspiracy of
the crucifixion by anti-Christ conspirators of the

Supreme Court in their denial of prayer and their betrayal of a nation."[26] Two people were killed and six
federal marshals were shot in the fifteen hours of riots
that followed. (Walker would later be arrested twice for
public lewdness in Dallas park bathrooms.)[27]

The rash of right-wing extremist groups from the explicitly military to overheated anti-communist compelled former President Eisenhower to speak out on the
subject in the early 1960s: "I don't think the United
States needs super-patriots," Ike gently scolded. "We
need patriotism, honestly practiced by all of us, and we
don't need these people [who pretend to be] more patriotic than you or anybody else."[28] President Kennedy
also weighed in, warning of "armed bands of civilian
guerrillas that are more likely to supply local vigilantes
than national vigilance."[29]   lost Patriotism

In the ensuing two decades, anti-government left-
wing extremist groups dominated headlines, but there
were outbursts of far-right violence such as the 1979 mas-
sacre in Greensboro, North Carolina, in which KKK and
American Nazi Party members shot and killed five leftist
protesters, including members of the Communist Workers
Party. The recession of the late 1970s and early '80s saw
the rise of the Posse Comitatus groups, which claimed
that the highest government authority lay with county
officials like sheriffs and that there had been a "subtle
subversion" of the U.S. Constitution that reflected a
"criminal conspiracy to obstruct justice, disfranchise citizens and liquidate the Constitutional Republic of these

United States."[30] By the the 1990s, America experienced the rise of the anti-government patriot militia movement, paramilitary groups featuring a mix of white pride and Christian identity politics, fueled by anger at the Bill Clinton–led federal government after deaths at Ruby Ridge and the Branch Davidian compound in Waco, Texas. The destruction of the Murrah Federal Building in Oklahoma City was the culmination of years of escalation, and subsequent scrutiny reduced the militia's momentum. But the Southern Poverty Law Center has tracked seventy-five plots, attacks and murders from far-right militia types in the years since Oklahoma City.[31]

In total, there were 845 acts of domestic terrorism from far-right and affiliated white supremacist groups between 1954 and 2004, including shootings, bombing and arson.[32] The record shows this is not a benign movement of patriots, but a dangerous strain of extremism with both a rap sheet and a body count.

Today's Hatriots are potentially even more dangerous because of their ability to recruit and radicalize more people via the Internet. Their job is made easier by Wingnut media heroes and even members of Congress who give comfort to their conspiracy theories.

Alex Jones's syndicated radio show and his Web sites Prison Planet and Info Wars are a clearing house of conspiracy theories from 9/11 to the New World Order—and a home to unhinged Hatriots eager for "information" they can't get elsewhere. A self-described paleo-conservative and "aggressive constitutionalist,"

Jones is so far right he's left, establishing himself at the vanguard of fright-wing politics.

"The answer to 1984 is 1776!" is a typical battle cry that endears him to the Hatriots. During the presidency of George W. Bush, Jones eagerly advanced the idea that the Bush administration and bankers were behind the destruction of the World Trade Center (with companion DVDs for sale). Now that Obama is in office, a whole new cottage industry of hate has opened up: He's selling semi-slick productions with titles like *The Fall of the Republic* and *The Obama Deception,* which are passed on like Grateful Dead bootlegs among the Hatriot underground. The pitch is always apocalypse, telling viewers "The last vestiges of our free republic are being swept away . . . the destiny of humanity is in our hands." The common ground is opposition to the federal storm troopers he sees as trying to impose one-world government on the few remaining patriots left. When Pittsburgh police engaged in modest riot control measures at a 2009 G-20 summit, Jones was ready to climb the ramparts, referring to the police as "complete enemies of America. . . . Our military's been taken over. . . . This is the end of our country. . . . They'd love to kill 10,000 Americans. . . .The republic is falling right now."[33]

Given his full-throated embrace of the crazy (always presented as a search for the truth), what's really troubling is that members of Congress go on Jones's radio show. Ron Paul is a frequent guest. Texas Republican Louie Gohmert chose the venue to say: "This socialist health care . . . is going to absolutely kill senior citizens. They'll put them on lists and force them to die early"[34] Florida Democrat Alan Grayson used the opportunity to call an aide to Federal Reserve chairman Ben Bernanke a "K-Street whore." Going on Jones's radio show isn't just a serious lapse of judgment, it seems to inspire serious lapses in judgment as well.

There is a trickle-down effect to hardworking people who identify with the message of anger and anxiety. The Oath Keeper–affiliated Nevada deli owner Billy Glassberg describes Alex Jones as his "hero": "He stands for the Constitution, for America and sovereignty. Regardless of whether you want to know something or not, you've got to investigate the truth. There's no more right and there's no more left. It's all about Americans and Globalists. That's it. And it was Globalists behind 9/11."[35]

His diner, Brooklyn Billy's, stands less than a mile from the Las Vegas Strip in sight of the Mandalay Bay Casino in the corner of an office park. Next to the sign in the window that boasts "the best pastrami west of New York" another reads "free speech zone." On the walls are posters of Robert De Niro as Travis Bickle in *Taxi Driver* and Al Pacino in *Scarface* bearing the slogan "Who I trust? I trust me." Framed on the opposite wall is a yellowing *New York Daily News* cover dated November 23, 1963. The headline blares "President Shot Dead." On the glass of the frame, Billy has written, "Killed by the N.W.O."—i.e., the New World Order.

Billy is friendly, unassuming. His mother works the register while he makes the sandwiches in back, listening to Alex Jones's radio show blaring out of the speakers.

Billy believes that "Obama should be tried for treason." But it's not personal. "He's a puppet in the New World Order. He picked up the ball where Bush left it. . . . As far as the Republican and Democratic Party, Parties, it's two sides of the same coin. They're all owned by the same bankers, whether it's the Rothschilds or the Morgans or the Rockefellers. . . . They put a black face on the New World Order because they know things are getting intense. They know people are starting to figure it out."

Like Alex Jones, Billy believes that 9/11 was an inside job. He says the planes hitting the towers were "remote controlled." What happened to the people on the planes, I ask. "What they do in black operations is incredible," Billy said. "I couldn't tell you what happened to the people on the planes." It wasn't bin Laden—"Al-Qaeda was formed by the CIA under the Carter Administration," he says.

Billy's bought into a topsy-turvy worldview where "the new definition for freedom is gonna be servitude." Obama's "job is to continue to destroy America for a world government. I mean it's so—it's so easy to understand. . . . It's sick. It's demented. But it's true."

But while Alex Jones is on the fright-wing fringe, Michael Savage reaches an audience of nine million people with his Hatriot-reinforcing predictions. "Martial law," he announced in 2009, "will be declared in this country over a pretext. I think the likelihood is very high that the gang that has taken over this country will declare . . . a pretext . . . the equivalent of the Reichstag fire [which helped the Nazis take over the German government] . . . to put in a form of martial law."[36]

Influential figures like Rush Limbaugh unwittingly add fuel to the Hatriot fire with his hyper-partisan exhortations: "If we just sit idly by and let Obama get all this stuff done, we're cooked. Because this is not just standard, left-wing politics. This is radical, left-wing Marxist socialism—fascism, whatever you want to call it. This is designed to forever remake the United States and to destroy the prosperity-generating capitalist system and private sector."

When Glenn Beck declares, "There is a coup going on. There is a stealing of America . . . done through the guise of an election,"[37] he is reaffirming Hatriot fears. And when Beck announces that "the government under Bush and under Obama . . . [is] slowly but surely moving us away from our republic and into a system of fascism," he is singing straight from the Hatriot hymnal without knowing it.

All this apocalyptic fearmongering has an impact on netroot "news" as well. In September, the conservative '09 magazine Newsmax.com had to pull down an online column from a regular contributor that imagined a "civilized" military coup "as a last resort to resolve the 'Obama problem.'" It was a rationale that echoed all the

Hatriot themes and fears from the Oath Keepers on down:

Officers swear to "support and defend the Constitution of the United States against all enemies, foreign and domestic." Unlike enlisted personnel, they do not swear to obey the orders of the president of the United States.

They can see that Americans are increasingly alarmed that this nation, under President Barack Obama, may not even be recognizable as America by the 2012 election . . .

Will the day come when patriotic general and flag officers sit down with the president, or with those who control him, and work out the national equivalent of a "family intervention," with some form of limited, shared responsibility?

Imagine a bloodless coup to restore and defend the Constitution through an interim administration that would do the serious business of governing and defending the nation. Skilled, military-trained, nation-builders would replace accountability-challenged, radical-left commissars.

Military intervention is what Obama's exponentially accelerating agenda for "fundamental change" toward a Marxist state is inviting upon America. A coup is not an ideal option, but Obama's radical ideal is not acceptable or reversible.[38]

In October, the idea of a coup was replaced by an online Hatriot call for revolution. A video anonymously posted on YouTube warned President Obama to "leave now and give us our country back." "If you stay," the message continued, "'We, The People' will systematically dismantle you, destroy you and reclaim what is rightfully ours. . . . We are angry and we are ready to take back the rights of the people. We will fight and we will win. . . . Dead line [sic] for your national response: October 15, 2009. Thank you to all patriots who support our cause. . . . Be prepared for when the fateful day of the declaration of war is nationally announced."[39]

There is an understandable tendency to dismiss the danger of the lone Wingnut whose posts dot Hatriot Web sites. Extreme rhetoric and talk about armed resistance is not the same thing as action. But history shows us that it is most often the lone gunman who takes hate-filled teachings to their ultimate extension of outright violence.

Oklahoma City bomber Timothy McVeigh, for example, was not a dedicated member of any one militia group. He was a wannabe, an outcast who felt rejected even by the militia men themselves. Likewise, the anarchist assassin of William McKinley, Leon Czolgosz, was not acting on the orders of an anarchist group. His fanaticism was so intense that he was thought to be a government agent and not welcomed into the anarchist circles of Chicago—not a generally discerning lot. The figure of the lone gunman was defined by the paranoid Marxist U.S. marine who moved to Moscow and then re-

defected, Lee Harvey Oswald. Even Eric Rudolph, the
Atlanta Olympic bomber driven by anti-abortion and
anti-gay beliefs, was influenced by indoctrination but
acted alone. These figures were darkly inspired by the
velocity of rhetoric around them.

The line between political fantasy and reality can
blur for the unhinged. Hatriot fears can have deadly
consequences, with a body count evident in the first six
months of 2009 alone.

On April 4, three Pittsburgh police officers were shot
and killed by Richard Andrew Poplawski, wearing body
armor and wielding a semi-automatic weapon. Poplawski
was a frequent visitor to Alex Jones's Web sites and a
poster on the white supremacist Stormfront.org, expressing fears that America is controlled by a cabal of Jews,
that U.S. soldiers would be used against American citizens and a ban on guns be imposed.[40]

On April 25, Joshua Cartwright, a Florida national
guardsman, shot and killed two Florida sheriff's
deputies as the officers attempted to arrest Cartwright
on domestic violence charges. In the police report Cartwright's wife said he "believed that the U.S. Government was conspiring against him. She said he had been
severely disturbed that Barack Obama had been elected
President."[41]

On May 31, Scott Roeder walked into a Wichita,
Kansas, church and shot and killed Dr. George Tiller,
who as part of his practice performed late-term abortions. Roeder was a member of the Posse Comitatus-

descended Freemen movement in the 1990s, which asserted its members were "sovereign citizens" not subject to federal law while African-Americans were "14th amendment citizens." In 1996, Roeder had been pulled over and found to have a pound of gunpowder attached to a nine-volt battery and a switch as well as blasting caps and bullets. The prosecutor in the case described him—accurately, as it turned out—as a "substantial threat to public safety."[42]

On June 10, James von Brunn, an eighty-eight-year-old neo-Nazi walked into the United States Holocaust Memorial Museum in Washington, D.C., killed a forty-year-old African-American security guard, Officer Stephen Tyrone Johns, and wounded several others. Von Brunn had previously served six years in prison for attempting to kidnap members of the Federal Reserve at gunpoint. A note left in his car read, "You want my weapons, this is how you'll get them . . . the Holocaust is a lie . . . Obama was created by Jews. Obama does what his Jew owners tell him to. Jews captured America's money. Jews control the mass media."[43]

The common Hatriot strains behind all these killings are more chilling when you consider that President Obama received more death threats in the months after his election than any president on record[44]—and he received Secret Service protection earlier than any presidential candidate because of repeated threats to his life. Some of the plots have been serious, others half-baked, while chat room comments about Obama's assassination are made almost offhand, such as an exchange on the draft-Palin site TeamSarah.com where one poster named Heather described Election Day as the "most terrible" in history and then asks "how long until obama is shot??????" To which a poster named Josie responded: "There are plenty of people that would like to see Obama end that way."[45]

So when you see militia groups recruiting at Tea Parties with signs that say "AK-47: Today's Pitchfork" or when a Washington, D.C., man is found to have an M-16 gun and two pistols which had been inscribed by a local gunsmith with the words "Christian Warrior" and "NoBama,"[46] it's worth being concerned.

There is a cost to the constant drumbeat that turns political opponents into personal enemies. All that's left is an unhinged soul who takes the hate as a call to heroism—the small but decisive step from being ready to die for a cause and being willing to kill for it. As one federal law enforcement agent, speaking anonymously of the Hatriots' rise, said: "All it's lacking is a spark. I think it's only a matter of time before you see threats and violence."[47]

CONCLUSION:
HOW TO TAKE AMERICA BACK
FROM THE LUNATIC FRINGE

We are allowing the Wingnuts to hijack our politics. It doesn't have to be this way.

At a time when the common sense center is under attack, we can take America back from the lunatic fringe. They may have networks and netroots, but we have the numbers. I'm talking about the non-screamers and the non-shouters, everyday Americans who care more about solving common problems than obsessively attacking political opponents. We can re-center our civic debate by declaring our independence from the far right and far left.

Wingnuts offer their fellow travelers the false comfort of rigid certainty in a changing world—dividing our country into good versus evil, us against them. Fundamentalism has a powerful appeal for people who feel powerless, especially when it gets dressed up as an ideology or attaches itself to a party label.

But when you pull the curtain back on Wingnut politics, behind the all-or-nothing demands, apocalyptic warnings and the addiction to self-righteous anger, you'll see that fear is the motivating factor: fear of the other; fear wrapped up in the American flag; fear calling itself freedom.

The Wingnuts are recycling scripts that are decades old. But it is not the language of the Founding Fathers, as they like to believe. The Founding Fathers warned about the dangers of faction—Wingnuts enflame it. The Founding Fathers were focused on uniting the nation—Wingnuts try to divide it.

They are selling the same old snake oil that merchants of political paranoia have been selling for most of American history.

The federal government has been accused of tyranny and trying to restrict states' rights since the debate to ratify the Constitution. It was the South's battle cry at the start of the Civil War, and it was the logic behind white resistance to Reconstruction and desegregation. It was the anxiety festering beneath militia explosions from Waco to the Oklahoma City bombing.

The specter of a sinister plot to create a one-world government goes back almost a century to fights over the League of Nations against the backdrop of the Bolshevik revolution. It was carried forward by the John Birch Society, which drew recruits with its talk of U.N. troops invading the United States through the southern border with the approval of alleged Manchurian candidate and Soviet spy Dwight D. Eisenhower.

Days before John F. Kennedy's assassination, 5,000 flyers were distributed in downtown Dallas, featuring

side-by-side photos of Kennedy in profile and face forward, like a mug shot. Below it read "WANTED FOR
TREASON" with this list of charges:[1]

- Betraying the Constitution (which he swore to uphold):
  He is turning sovereignty of the U.S. over to the
  communist controlled United Nations: He is betraying
  our friends . . . and befriending our enemies.
- He has been WRONG on innumerable issues affecting
  the security of the U.S. (United Nations—Berlin Wall—
  missile removal—Cuba—weak deals—test ban treaty,
  etc.).
- He has given support and encouragement to the
  Communist-inspired racial riots.
- He has illegally invaded a sovereign State with federal
  troops.
- He has consistently appointed Anti-Christians to Federal
  office: Upholds the Supreme Court in its Anti-Christian
  rulings. Aliens and known Communists abound in
  federal offices.
- He has been caught in fantastic lies to the American
  people.

These accusations still echo from Wingnuts today.
Obama is accused of betraying the Constitution and
turning national sovereignty over to the U.N. He is accused of selling out allies in favor of talks with Iran and
Russia while making our nation less safe. He is accused
of giving support and encouragement to radical leftist

groups and is seen by some as being the product of not just the civil rights era but of communist influencers. From the Oath Keepers to the Tenthers, the specter of federal troops illegally invading sovereign states is raised. Obama is seen by some as anti-Christian, even Muslim, and accused of appointing radical secularists and communists to federal office. And the Birthers see a sinister plot by Obama to hide his true identity as an illegal alien Manchurian candidate.

Beneath it all is a fear that America is fragile and that our democracy can be undone in a few easy steps. These professed patriots do not have faith in the strength of the American system they want to preserve. Wingnut fervor is no longer isolated because of the Internet, and formerly fringe figures now have national reach. Political parties are held hostage by their most extreme voices, while the rise of partisan media pumps up political divisions. It's an old problem—"the best lack all conviction, while the worst are full of passionate intensity," as the poet William Butler Yeats once wrote—but it's taken on new urgency.

We cannot hope to change human nature. There will always be cranks and conspiracy theorists among us. But we can try to improve things—we don't have to accept the debasement of civil discourse or civic decline. We can take steps to ensure that the lunatic fringe remains on the fringe and stops bleeding into the base and then poisoning the mainstream.

First, we have the numbers on our side—more Americans are independents than Democrats or Republicans, and more Americans are centrist than liberal or conservative. Americans are not deeply divided—our political parties, pundits and activists are—and the explosive growth of independent voters is a direct reaction to this disconnect. If more Americans declare their independence from the extremists on both sides and organize across party lines, we can determine who wins elections—and move our nation not left or right, but forward.

Second, we need to change the rules of the game—the professional partisans have rigged the system to re-elect incumbents by creating closed-primary safe seats that empower the extremes. If we enact nonpartisan redistricting reform with competitive general elections and open primaries, it will have a calming effect on our contorted civic discourse. It will empower the moderate majority rather than the Wingnut extremes. No single action would do more to heal the harsh but artificial polarization of American politics.

Third, we need to stand up against the extremes, playing offense not defense. And that's been a big part of the problem to date—the moderate majority of Americans has been bullied into intimidated silence. It's time to straighten our civic backbone and be the honest brokers in politics, punching both left and right as conscience and common sense dictate.

Taken together, it's a declaration of independence—a determination to view politics not simply in terms of right versus left, but right versus wrong. It means having a healthy skepticism and a sense of humor when confronted with ideological certainty. It means rejecting the reflexive defense of the indefensible when it comes from someone on your "team." Ironically, the parties have an interest in this as well—they cannot be held hostage by their most extreme wings and hope to win broad durable mandates.

In the process, we can hold the extremes accountable while restoring a missing sense of perspective and balance to our politics. A lack of perspective is the tell-tale sign of the Wingnut. When we throw around terms like dictatorship and tyranny in American politics to score partisan points we debase ourselves and our history.

There's a final irony in the Wingnut Wars that also contains a hint of hope—everyone thinks they are fighting for freedom.

Conservatives see the threat of big government's taxing and spending as an assault not just on economic freedom but also on individual freedom. Liberals believe they are fighting for individual freedom in their struggle for civil rights and reproductive rights.

Everyone thinks they are the true patriots. Everyone finds a way to convince themselves that they are the inheritors and defenders of the American Revolution. And in an implicit acknowledgement of Americans' allergy to extremism, each side tries to paint their opponents as the real extremists. In this sense, we are not all that far apart.

And so maybe a final word from the original Founding Father can help get us back on the same page. Wingnuts often try to pretend that there is nothing more American than high-pitched, no-holds-barred ideological battle. But in his Farewell Address, George Washington made it clear that he perceived no greater threat to the American experiment than a partisan demagogue who "agitates the community with ill-founded jealousies and false alarms, kindles the animosity of one part against another."[2]

Washington was the original independent. He belonged to no political party as a matter of principle and warned against those who "serve to organize faction, to give it an artificial and extraordinary force; to put, in the place of the delegated will of the nation the will of a party." And while Washington was enough of a realist to recognize that the rise of political parties was inevitable, he tried to tell future generations that "the common and continual mischiefs of the spirit of party are sufficient to make it the interest and duty of a wise people to discourage and restrain it." After all, as Washington wrote, "the alternate domination of one faction over another, sharpened by the spirit of revenge, natural to party dissension, which in different ages and countries has perpetrated the most horrid enormities, is itself a frightful despotism."

George Washington warned us about the Wingnuts. We would be wise to take his advice.

ACKNOWLEDGMENTS

This book was written in three months, bridged by my wedding and honeymoon. So it should be no surprise that it is dedicated to my bride, Margaret, who showed superhuman support and patience during the process. She is beautiful and bright in every way and I am blessed to call her my bride.

It's an honor to be the first imprint for Beast Books and I owe a deep debt of gratitude to Tina Brown, Harold Evans and my colleagues at The Daily Beast who helped me move the ball down the field at great speed. I am especially appreciative to Edward Felsenthal, Randall Lane, Rebecca Fox, Andrew Kirk, Christine Marra and the team at Perseus. My research assistants were also essential in getting the book done and documented on time, including Denver Nicks, Stephen Brown and Ahmed Salim. And special thanks goes to my literary agent, Ed Victor. At CNN, the Wingnuts of the Week segment took off because of the support and encouragement of Kiran Chetry, Janelle Rodriguez, John Roberts, Jamie Kraft, Karrah Kaplan, Alexis Ginsburg, Derek Dodge and everyone at *American Morning*.

I want to thank my parents, John and Dianne Avlon—their love, support and encouragement have always been invaluable. My in-laws Andy and Jeanie Hoover have been warm and welcoming (and Andy, just to be clear, you're *not* a Wingnut) as have my new brother and sister-in-law, Alex and Margaret. I've been blessed with a wonderful family: my grandmother Toula Phillips, Aunts Joan and Lexa, Uncles Alex and David, my brother, Reynolds, and cousin Alex Timbers. My godfather, Peter John, and godmother, Elaine, as well as my own godchildren, Alexandra Catlin, Catherine Vanderzee, and Benjamin, Flora and Matilda Damon—and all our friends down in Charleston. I want to thank my best man, Jay Vanderzee, as well as my groomsmen Mike Jackson, George Catlin, Jesse Angelo, Owen Brennan, Eric DelBalso, Howard Gould, Jamie Schriebl and Matt Lockwood. Special thanks also go out to Matt Pottinger (USMC), Rich Wager, the Policy Team: Dan Freedman, Jayson White, Jen Pollom, Chris Coffey, Jemma Futterman and Marco DeSena; Bill Simon, the Manhattan Institute, Dave Maney, Dave Dunbar, Frank Barry, Dick Dadey, Alan Dobrin, Peggy Noonan, Suzanne Robinson, Bobby Grossman and Erik Sorenson. Many people were generous with their interview time, including David Frum (who sparked the concept of white minority politics), Joe Scarborough, Rich Lowry, Charles Johnson, Kathleen Parker, and Mark Potok of the Southern Poverty Legal Center.

On language, I should note that some in the netroots believe the term "Wingnut" should apply exclusively to the far right. "Moonbat" is the preferred label for folks on the far left in this worldview. But this distinction seems to split the difference along partisan lines, where I generally and genuinely believe that the far right and far left can be equally insane and so deserve the same word to describe them. No discrimination here.

For further background reading on the broad subject of homegrown extremism and how to overcome it, I'd recommend Richard Hofstadter's classic *The Paranoid Style in American Politics,* Harry and Bonaro Overstreet's early '60s snapshot *The Strange Tactics of Extremism,* Arthur Schlesinger, Jr.'s *The Disuniting of America,* Morris Fiorina's *Culture War? The Myth of a Polarized America* and Cass Sunstein's *Going to Extremes: How Like Minds Unite and Divide.*

NOTES

Introducing the Wingnuts

1. http://mediamatters.org/mmtv/200904210014

2. http://www.newsbusters.org/blogs/kyle-drennen/2009/09/24/msnbcs-ed-shultz-erupts-republicans-want-see-you-dead

3. http://www.lvrj.com/news/oath-keepers-pledges-to-prevent-dictatorship-in-united-states-64690232.html

4. http://www.nytimes.com/2009/11/08/magazine/08Armey-t.html

5. http://mediamatters.org/mmtv/200909230021

6. http://www.youtube.com/watch?v=h5qWFHzwAz8

7. http://www.huffingtonpost.com/2009/06/03/rush-limbaugh-claims-obam_n_211162.html

8. http://www.nytimes.com/2009/12/06/us/06threat.html

9. Christopher Hewitt, *Political Violence and Terrorism in Modern America: A Chronology* (Santa Barbara, CA: Praeger Security International, 2005), pp. 28-90.

10. Richard Hofstadter, *The Paranoid Style in American Politics* (New York: Vintage Books, 2008), pp. 23-24.

11. http://washingtonindependent.com/61229/more-trent-franks-the-president-is-an-enemy-of-humanity

12. http://thehill.com/blogs/blog-briefing-room/news/64173-grayson-republicans-are-the-enemy-of-america

13. http://blog.cleveland.com/openers/2008/01/ad_watch_barack_obamas_inspiri.html

14. http://thepage.time.com/obamas-new-stump-speech/

15. http://www.issues2000.org/Senate/John_McCain_Civil_Rights.htm

16. http://politicalticker.blogs.cnn.com/2008/06/21/obama-theyre-going-to-try-to-make-you-afraid-of-me/

17. http://www.cnn.com/ELECTION/2008/results/polls/#USP00p1

18. http://www.clarusrg.com/ELECTIONRECAP.pdf

19. http://www.politico.com/blogs/glennthrush/0709/58_of_GOP_not_suredont_believe_Obama_born_in_US.html?showall

20. http://www.washingtonpost.com/ac2/wp-dyn?pagename= article&contentId=A37125-2003Dec4.

21. http://www.fec.gov/pubrec/2000presgeresults.htm

22. http://www.fightbacknews.org/2001fall/nowar.htm

23. http://www.dailykos.com/story/2005/9/28/152665/-Why-We-Hate-George-W.-Bush

24. http://www.cbsnews.com/stories/2005/11/02/national/main1005030.shtml

25. http://www.npr.org/templates/story/story.php?storyId=16422285

26. http://www.youtube.com/watch?v=u19KHbTJEOk

27. http://www.msnbc.msn.com/id/10767465/

28. http://seattletimes.nwsource.com/html/localnews/2002981541_sheehan09.html

29. http://www.breitbart.tv/?p=2973

30. Fox News, "Hannity & Colmes," September 26, 2005.

31. 2008 ANES (American National Election Studies) National Election Study.

32. http://people-press.org/report/?pageid=1516

33. William Safire, *Safire's New Political Dictionary* (New York: Random House, 1993), p. 453.

Of Tea Parties and Town Halls

1. http://www.cnbc.com/id/15840232?video=1039849853

2. http://www.myfoxchicago.com/dpp/news/TeaParty

3. http://rpc.senate.gov/public/_files/042909100DaysofBailoutsand MakingaBadSituationWorse.pdf

4. http://money.cnn.com/2009/01/28/news/economy/house_vote_wednesday/index.htm?postversion=2009012819

5. http://hotair.com/archives/2009/02/25/house-passes-410-billion-spending-bill-as-obama-prepares-634-billion-health-care-fund/

6. http://www.fivethirtyeight.com/2009/04/tea-party-nonpartisan-attendance.html

7. http://politics.theatlantic.com/2009/07/lawmakers_will_face_tea_parties_and_more_in_august.php

8. http://mediamatters.org/research/200904170011

9. http://gatewaypundit.blogspot.com/2009/07/rep-conyers-why-bother-to-read-health.html

10. http://thinkprogress.org/2009/08/05/freshman-dem-assaulted/

11. http://www.talkingpointsmemo.com/documents/2009/08/memo-details-co-ordinated-anti-reform-harrassment-strategy.php?page=1

12. http://www.talkingpointsmemo.com/documents/2009/08/memo-details-co-ordinated-anti-reform-harrassment-strategy.php?page=1

13. http://tpmdc.talkingpointsmemo.com/2009/08/protestor-in-connecticut-treat-dodd-with-handful-of-painkillers-and-whiskey.php

14. http://www.adl.org/special_reports/rage-grows-in-America/Rage-Grows-In-America.pdf

15. http://www.columbiamissourian.com/stories/2009/08/11/mccaskill-admonishes-crowd-forum/

16. http://www.facebook.com/note.php?note_id=113851103434

17. http://tpmdc.talkingpointsmemo.com/2009/08/americans-for-prosperity-compares-health-care-reform-to-holocaust-tells-protesters-to-put-fear-of-go.php?ref=fpblg

18. http://www.politicsdaily.com/2009/08/25/john-mccain-booed-for-saying-obama-respects-the-constitution

19. http://motherjones.com/politics/2009/12/tempest-tea-party

20. http://www.cnn.com/2009/POLITICS/09/12/tea.party.express/index.html

21. Ibid.

22. Ibid.

23. http://www.wtsp.com/news/local/story.aspx?storyid=111086&catid=8

24. http://tpmdc.talkingpointsmemo.com/2009/08/town-halls-turning-into-town-brawls.php

25. http://www.youtube.com/watch?v=3fHSW4Txxz8

26. http://www.cnn.com/2009/POLITICS/09/12/tea.party.express/index.html

Obama Derangement Syndrome

1. http://www.grassfire.org/111/about.htm

2. http://siteanalytics.compete.com/grassfire.org/

3. http://crooksandliars.com/john-amato/fox-website-commenter-wants-assassinate

4. http://www.freerepublic.com/focus/bloggers/2127465/posts

5. http://www.newsweek.com/id/195085

6. http://www.foxnews.com/wires/2008Nov15/0,4670,ObamaThreats,00.html

7. http://www.foxnews.com/printer_friendly_wires/2008Nov10/
0,4675,CongressmanObamaMarxist,00.html

8. http://www.msnbc.msn.com/id/27705755/

9. http://www.foxnews.com/wires/2008Nov15/
0,4670,ObamaThreats,00.html

10. http://rawstory.com/news/2008/Idaho_students_chant_
assassinate_Obama_on_1112.html

11. http://themoderatevoice.com/44879/arizona-pastor-repeats-
wish-for-barack-obamas-death/

12. http://blogs.phoenixnewtimes.com/bastard/2009/08/tempe_
pastor_steven_anderson_p.php

13. http://www.youtube.com/watch?v=f8NJPsj5kdU

14. http://mediamatters.org/mmtv/200802250008

15. http://mediamatters.org/research/200802130016?f=h_latest

16. http://thinkprogress.org/2008/07/29/krauthammer-obama-nazis/

17. http://mediamatters.org/research/200807240001

18. http://mediamatters.org/research/200804040005

19. http://weblogs.sun-sentinel.com/news/politics/broward/blog/
2008/10/republican_creator_of_sign_lik_1.html

20. http://weblogs.sun-sentinel.com/news/politics/broward/blog/
2008/10/republican_creator_of_sign_lik_1.html

21. http://www.breitbart.com/article.php?id=D94CDDM80&show_
article=1

22. http://mediamatters.org/limbaughwire/2009/08/19

23. http://www.nytimes.com/2009/04/20/us/politics/20caucus.html

24. http://thinkprogress.org/2009/04/01/beck-march-to-Fascism/

25. http://thinkprogress.org/2009/06/23/md-gop-obama-hitler/

26 http://gawker.com/5340436/meet-pamela-pilger-the-crazy-lady-
who-yelled-heil-hitler-at-a-jewish-supporter-of-health-care-reform

27. http://www.washingtonmonthly.com/archives/individual/2009_
12/021407.php

28. http://www.mountvernonnews.com/local/09/09/22/
controversial-float-meant-to-inspire-citizen-voices

29. http://www.mountvernonnews.com/local/09/09/22/
controversial-float-meant-to-inspire-citizen-voices

30. http://tpmdc.talkingpointsmemo.com/2009/09/former-bush-
administration-official-warns-against-economic-fascism-under-obama.
php

31. Ibid.

32. http://www.politico.com/news/stories/1009/27986.html#ixzz0
TJGDPKVR

33. http://seattletimes.nwsource.com/html/politics/2009882084_
gasparian16m.html

34. http://www.cuttingedge.org/news/n1315.cfm

35. http://www.wnd.com/index.php?pageId=79411

36. http://blogs.abcnews.com/politicalradar/2008/10/palin-invokes-
s.html

37. http://blogs.abcnews.com/politicalpunch/2008/06/delay-obamas-
a.html

38. http://thinkprogress.org/2008/10/20/marxist-fascist/

39. http://articles.baltimoresun.com/1992-06-25/news/1992177016_
1_spiro-agnew-ha-ha-ha-quayle

40. http://corner.nationalreview.com/post/?q=NmM2NDQ3ZWQ1
YWM0Y2QyZTUxMDdkY2M2OTJlNGE5MWE=

41. http://www.huffingtonpost.com/casey-ganemccalla/top-10-
obama-player-hater_b_152490.html_NoPara

42. http://news.yahoo.com/s/politico/20081207/pl_politico/16257

43. http://crooksandliars.com/david-neiwert/beck-obama-has-us-
road-not-just-soci

44. http://new.khastv.com/modules/news/article.php?storyid=
16300

45. http://www.scrippsnews.com/node/37045

46. http://www.charlotteobserver.com/408/story/228317.html

47. http://www.newsweek.com/id/169192

48. http://www.newsweek.com/id/169192

49. http://www.snopes.com/politics/obama/antichrist.asp

50. http://www.sltrib.com/faith/ci_10859898

51. http://www.time.com/time/nation/article/0,8599,1830590,00.
html?iid=sphere-inline-sidebar

52. http://www.time.com/time/nation/article/0,8599,1830590,00.
html?iid=sphere-inline-sidebar

53. http://www.glennbeck.com/content/articles/article/198/7060/

54. http://www.sltrib.com/faith/ci_10859898

55. http://www.newsweek.com/id/169192

56. http://publicpolicypolling.blogspot.com/2009/09/extremism-in-
new-jersey.html

The Birth of White Minority Politics

1. http://newsbusters.org/blogs/noel-sheppard/2009/04/16/garofalo-tea-partiers-are-all-racists-who-hate-black-president

2. Bureau of Labor Statistics, "Current Population Survey—November 2009."

3. http://www.census.gov/PressRelease/www/releases/archives/population/001720.html

4. Richard Hofstadter, *The Paranoid Style in American Politics,* Vintage Books, pp. 23–24.

5. http://mediamatters.org/columns/200912110041

6. http://mediamatters.org/mmtv/200908210049

7. http://www.wnd.com/index.php?pageId=113463

8. http://www.humanevents.com/article.php?id=32654

9. http://buchanan.org/blog/is-america-coming-apart-2159

10. In *The Civil War,* Ken Burns's PBS documentary.

11. http://912dc.org/2009/08/continental-soldiers-wanted-for-9-12-march/

12. http://voices.washingtonpost.com/44/2008/10/17/palin_clarifies_her_pro-americ.html

13. http://articles.latimes.com/2008/apr/13/nation/na-obama13

14. http://latimesblogs.latimes.com/washington/2008/10/john-mccain-bac.html

15. http://www.yelp.com/topic/los-angeles-al-jazeera-exposes-racism-at-sarah-palin-rally-in-ohio

16. http://www.youtube.com/watch?v=NtZWwgw__WY

17. http://latimesblogs.latimes.com/washington/2008/10/fox-news-execut.html

18. http://elections.nytimes.com/2008/results/president/exit-polls.html

19. http://ap.google.com/article/ALeqM5gGwsssa7xKHFgjdLsgtE...

20. http://www.nationaljournal.com/njmagazine/nj_20091010_1507.php

21. Eric Foner, *Reconstruction: America's Unfinished Revolution, 1863–1877* (New York: HarperCollins, 1988, 2002), p. 198.

22. Ibid., p. 551.

23. John B. Judis, *William F. Buckley, Jr., Patron Saint of the Conservatives* (New York: Simon and Schuster, 2001), p. 138.

24. Foner, *Reconstruction,* p. 251.

25. http://www.strom.clemson.edu/strom/bio.html

26. *National Review,* January 25, 1956, p. 5.

27. Barry Goldwater, *The Conscience of a Conservative* (new edition; Princeton University Press, 2007), p. 28

28. http://gawker.com/5380714/gop-tries-to-claim-the-ghost-of-jackie-robinson

29. http://www.washingtonpost.com/wp-dyn/content/article/2008/01/14/AR2008011402079.html

30. http://www.nytimes.com/1998/12/27/weekinreview/impeachment-republicans-130-years-later-dueling-with-the-heirs-of-jeff-davis.html

31. http://transcripts.cnn.com/TRANSCRIPTS/0907/10/ltm.01.html

32. Ibid.

33. http://www.thedailybeast.com/blogs-and-stories/2009-07-11/young-gop-chooses-hate

34. http://www.thedailybeast.com/blogs-and-stories/2009-07-06/new-gop-racist-headache/

35. http://www.arktimes.com/blogs/arkansasblog/audrasiglershay.doc

36. *American Jewish Year Book.* (New York: American Jewish Committee, 1967).

37. http://indian.senate.gov/exhibits.pdf

38. http://leonardosnotebook.blogspot.com/2008/11/on-airing-untoward-comments.html

39. http://www.tampabay.com/news/localgovernment/article973693.ece

40. http://www.msnbc.msn.com/id/29423045/

41. http://www.huffingtonpost.com/2009/06/14/rusty-depass-south-caroli_n_215439.html

42. http://www.huffingtonpost.com/2009/06/16/tennessee-gop-staffer-ema_n_216085.html

43. http://tpmmuckraker.talkingpointsmemo.com/2009/07/conservative_activist_forwards_racist_pic_showing.php

44. http://blog.newsweek.com/blogs/thegaggle/archive/2009/10/26/more-rnc-internet-follies-racist-images-on-fan-photo-page.aspx

45. http://www.commercialappeal.com/news/2009/dec/04/mayor-fires-at-obama-online/

46. http://www.thedailybeast.com/blogs-and-stories/2009-07-13/the-gops-vote-for-hatemdashand-suicide/

Polarizing for Profit

1. http://people-press.org/reports/pdf/444.pdf

2. http://people-press.org/reports/pdf/444.pdf

3. Cass R. Sunstein, *Going to Extremes* (New York: Oxford University Press, 2009), p. 4.

4. Hofstadter, *The Paranoid Style in American Politics,* pp. 29–30.

5. Interview with the author, 10/15/09.

6. http://www.arbitron.com/downloads/radiotoday08.pdf

7. http://www.frumforum.com/talk-radio-gets-angrier-as-its-revenues-drop

8. Ibid.

9. Interview with the author, 10/16/09.

10. http://www.politico.com/news/stories/1209/30231.html

11. http://www.politico.com/news/stories/1209/30231.html

12. Interview with the author, 11/4/09.

13. http://www.politicsdaily.com/2009/12/29/the-gops-ugly-2010-campaign-pushing-the-obacalypse/

14. Glenn Beck, *The Real America* (New York: Pocket Books, 2005), p. 2.

15. http://www.glennbeck.com/content/tv/

16. http://www.huffingtonpost.com/2009/11/09/glenn-beck-publisher-clai_n_351184.html

17. http://mediamatters.org/blog/200909110032

18. http://www.glennbeck.com/content/articles/article/198/33398/?ck=1

19. Beck, *The Real America,* p. 194.

20. http://www.salon.com/news/feature/2009/09/22/glenn_beck_two/print.html

21. Beck, *The Real America,* p. 53.

22. http://www.salon.com/news/feature/2009/09/23/glenn_beck_three/

23. http://mediamatters.org/mmtv/200903040029

24. Ibid.

25. http://mediamatters.org/mmtv/200903310037

26. http://mediamatters.org/mmtv/200904020037

27. http://mediamatters.org/mmtv/200907270008

28. http://mediamatters.org/mmtv/200907210041

29. http://mediamatters.org/mmtv/200907220015

30. http://mediamatters.org/mmtv/200904130030

31. http://mediamatters.org/mmtv/200904070026

32. http://mediamatters.org/mmtv/200907280008

33. http://mediamatters.org/mobile/research/200906120029

34. http://mediamatters.org/mmtv/200908310007

35. http://www.stormfront.org/forum/showthread.php?s=
5f77bb3973594fd6147d499bc9073207&p=7213067#post7213067

36. http://www.stormfront.org/forum/showthread.php?t=
629488&page=13

37. http://www.stormfront.org/forum/showpost.php?p=7211864&
postcount=69

38. http://www.stormfront.org/forum/showpost.php?p=7214009&
postcount=111

39. http://www.usatoday.com/sports/2005-06-13-olbermann-espn_
x.htm

40. http://www.salon.com/news/sports/col/olbermann/2002/11/17/
meaculpa/index.html

41. http://www.thenation.com/doc/20071008/kitman

42. http://www.huffingtonpost.com/2008/11/10/keith-olbermann-
does-the_n_142749.html

43. http://crooksandliars.com/2006/08/30/keith-olbermann-delivers-
one-hell-of-a-commentary-on-rumsfeld#comment-6

44. http://www.msnbc.msn.com/id/15392701/ns/msnbc_tv-
countdown_with_keith_olbermann/page/2/

45. http://www.msnbc.msn.com/id/15321167/

46. http://www.msnbc.msn.com/id/17351284/print/1/displaymode/
1098/

47. http://www.adl.org/media_watch/tv/20060728-MSNBC.htm

48. http://www.playboy.com/articles/playboy-interview-keith-
olbermann/index.html?page=2

49. http://www.msnbc.msn.com/id/30109453/

50. http://www.msnbc.msn.com/id/34455168/

51. http://www.msnbc.msn.com/id/34430893/ns/msnbc_tv-
countdown_with_keith_olbermann/

52. http://newsbusters.org/blogs/brad-wilmouth/2009/10/13/
olbermann-without-fascistic-hatred-malkin-just-mashed-bag-meat-
lipsti#ixzz0cMrII4Tc

53. http://pol.moveon.org/petraeus.html

54. http://www.dailykos.com/comments/2004/4/1/144156/3224

55. http://articles.latimes.com/2009/aug/30/nation/na-ticket30

56. http://www.conservapedia.com

57. http://www.colbertnation.com/the-colbert-report-videos/24039/october-17-2005/the-word—-truthiness

58. http://www.alexa.com/siteinfo/worldnetdaily.com

59. http://www.wnd.com/index.php?pageId=76022

60. http://www.wnd.com/index.php?pageId=61631

61. http://www.wnd.com/news/article.asp?ARTICLE_ID=59600

62. http://www.wnd.com/index.php?pageId=107588

63. http://www.wnd.com/index.php?fa=PAGE.view&pageId=106559

64. http://www.wnd.com/index.php?fa=PAGE.view&pageId=56626

65. http://www.wnd.com/news/article.asp?ARTICLE_ID=60020

66. http://www.wnd.com/index.php?pageId=63076

67. http://www.wnd.com/index.php?fa=PAGE.view&pageId=118710

68. http://www.wnd.com/index.php?fa=PAGE.view&pageId=118592

69. http://www.survivalseedbank.com/

70. http://www.wnd.com/index.php?pageId=86469

71. http://www.publicdiplomacy.org/1.htm

72. http://people-press.org/report/543/

73. http://www.washingtonpost.com/wp-dyn/articles/A56330-2005Jan7.html

74. http://www.independentnation.org/articles/ending_split_scream.htm

75. http://thinkprogress.org/2009/06/04/smith-media-bias-threat/

76. http://people-press.org/report/?pageid=1516

77. http://www.timepolls.com/hppolls/archive/poll_results_417.html

Sarah Palin and the Limbaugh Brigades

1. http://www.gallup.com/poll/124097/Huckabee-Romney-Palin-See-Most-Republican-Support-12.aspx

2. http://dyn.politico.com/printstory.cfm?uuid=263CFBB5-18FE-70B2-A8FB06C75393474D

3. http://www.breitbart.com/article.php?id=D93KD6Q00&show_article=1

4. http://voices.washingtonpost.com/44/2008/10/17/palin_clarifies_her_pro-americ.html

5. http://www.cbsnews.com/blogs/2008/10/19/politics/fromtheroad/entry4531388.shtml

6. http://www.huffingtonpost.com/2008/10/08/david-brooks-sarah-palin_n_133001.html

7. http://article.nationalreview.com/?q=MDZiMDhjYTU1NmI5Y2MwZjg2MWNiMWMyYTUxZDkwNTE=

8. http://www.cnn.com/2008/POLITICS/10/25/palin.tension/index.html

9. "Misconceptions of Obama Fuel Republican Campaign," October 13, 2008, Al-Jazeera.

10. http://www.nytimes.com/2008/10/31/us/politics/31poll.html?_r=2&scp=1&sq=palin%20%20poll&st=Search

11. http://www.rasmussenreports.com/premium_content/econ_crosstabs/october_2008/crosstabs_fox_variety_october_31_ november_1_2008

12. http://www.time.com/time/politics/article/0,8599,1846443,00.html

13. http://www.huffingtonpost.com/geoffrey-dunn/watermelon-roll-more-rac_b_152743.html_NoPara

14. http://mediamatters.org/mobile/research/200908100054

15. http://www.washingtonpost.com/wp-dyn/content/article/2009/11/29/AR2009112902717.html

16. http://publicpolicypolling.blogspot.com/2009/08/who-do-birthers-love.html

17. http://www.swamppolitics.com/news/politics/blog/2009/12/sarah_palin_birther_not_me_but.html

18. http://www.rushlimbaugh.com/home/daily/site_112009/content/01125110.guest.html

19. http://www.telegraph.co.uk/news/worldnews/2236873/US-talk-radio-host-Rush-Limbaugh-signs-400m-contract.html

20. http://www.sacbee.com/opinion/story/2324415.html

21. http://www.gallup.com/poll/114163/limbaugh-liked-not-republicans.aspx

22. http://www.rushlimbaugh.com/home/daily/site_011609/content/01125113.guest.html

23. http://www.newsweek.com/id/188279/page/2

24. http://www.politico.com/news/stories/0309/19460.html

25. http://www.politico.com/news/stories/0309/19517.html#ixzz0
UiBZfSRx

26. http://www.centerforpolitics.org/crystalball/article.php?id=
LJS2006031601

27. http://www.huffingtonpost.com/2008/10/17/gop-rep-channels-
mccarthy_n_135735.html

28. http://www.startribune.com/politics/national/house/41719957.
html?elr=KArksLckD8EQDUoaEyqyP4O:DW3ckUiD3aPc:_Yyc:aUUsZ

29. http://www.mcclatchydc.com/100/story/74549.html

30. http://coloradoindependent.com/36840/bachmann-slit-our-
wrists-be-blood-brothers'-to-beat-health-care-reform

31. http://tpmdc.talkingpointsmemo.com/2009/03/bachmann-blasts-
obamas-economic-marxism-calls-for-revolution-to-save-freedom.php

32. http://thinkprogress.org/2009/07/27/gohmert-conspiracies-
alexjones/

33. http://tpmdc.talkingpointsmemo.com/2009/10/debating-hate-
crimes-gohmert-rambles-on-about-bestiality-sex-with-corpses-voting-
for-a-black-man.php?ref=mp

34. http://www.spencerdailyreporter.com/story/1316727.html

35. http://www.house.gov/apps/list/hearing/ia05_king/col_
20060505_bite.html

36. http://www.politico.com/news/stories/0909/27266.html

37. http://rawstory.com/2009/10/grayson-fox-enemy-of-america/

38. http://www.washingtoncitypaper.com/blogs/sexist/2009/10/27/
sorry-alan-grayson-k-street-whore-isnt-specific-enough/

39. http://blogs.orlandosentinel.com/news_politics/2009/12/
grayson-wants-to-send-critic-to-jail-for-five-years.html

40. http://www.huffingtonpost.com/2009/09/29/gop-rep-trent-
franks-call_n_302713.html

41. http://www.cbsnews.com/blogs/2009/09/28/politics/
politicalhotsheet/entry5346428.shtml

42. http://washingtonindependent.com/61131/in-photos-the-how-
to-take-back-america-conference

43. http://www.stlbeacon.org/nation/leaders_at_conservative_
conference_call_for_tougher_talk_against_abortion_gays

44. http://washingtonindependent.com/61037/bachmann-in-st-
louis-defund-the-left-beware-one-world-currency

45. http://www.cbsnews.com/blogs/2009/09/28/politics/
politicalhotsheet/entry5346428.shtml

46. http://canadafreepress.com/index.php/article/15130

47. http://www.massresistance.org/docs/gen/09c/StLouis_conference/index.html

48. http://www.politico.com/news/stories/0909/27342_Page2.html#ixzz0TU0UH2VD

49. http://tpmdc.talkingpointsmemo.com/2009/09/the-values-voter-summit-a-celebration-of-the-religious-right.php#more

Hunting for Heretics

1. http://www.youtube.com/watch?v=tECGRppIj3w&feature=player_embedded

2. http://www.thedailybeast.com/blogs-and-stories/2009-04-28/specters-shocking-defection/

3. http://thinkprogress.org/2009/10/26/gingrich-beck-limbaugh/

4. http://www.examiner.com/x-25218-Dallas-Political-Buzz-Examiner~y2009m10d27-Newt-Gingrich—King-of-the-RINOs

5. http://thecaucus.blogs.nytimes.com/2009/11/23/gop-considers-purity-resolution-for-candidates/

6. http://search.opinionarchives.com/Summary/AmericanSpectator/V35I6P32-1.htm

7. http://www.rightprinciples.com/rino.html

8. Clive Webb, *Massive Resistance: Southern Opposition to the Second Reconstruction* (New York: Oxford University Press, 2005), p. 22.

9. Harry and Bonaro Overstreet, *The Strange Tactics of Extremism* (New York: Norton, 1964), p. 27.

10. http://www.calbuzz.com/tag/ken-khachigian/

11. http://www.nytimes.com/2001/03/19/us/conservatives-savor-their-role-as-insiders-at-the-white-house.html

12. www.justice.gov/oig/special/s0807/chapter3.htm

13. http://www.thedailybeast.com/blogs-and-stories/2009-01-15/how-i-got-interrogated-by-the-bushies/2/

14. http://www.thedailybeast.com/blogs-and-stories/2008-10-10/the-conservative-case-for-obama/

15. http://www.newsweek.com/id/188279

16. Interview with the author, 10/14/09.

17. http://article.nationalreview.com/?q=MDZiMDhjYTU1NmI5Y2MwZjg2MWNiMWMyYTUxZDkwNTE=

18. Interview with the author, 10/14/09.

19. http://www.thedailybeast.com/blogs-and-stories/2008-10-10/the-conservative-case-for-obama

20. Address of Governor Ronald Reagan to California Republican Assembly, Lafayette Hotel, Long Beach, April 1, 1967.

21. http://www.washingtontimes.com/news/2009/nov/24/conservatives-seek-reagan-litmus-test-for-rnc-fund/

22. http://www.nytimes.com/2009/05/11/us/politics/11cheney.html

23. http://www.independent.co.uk/news/from-lunatic-to-luminary-1156281.html

24. http://www.cnn.com/ALLPOLITICS/1998/05/29/goldwater.obit/

25. http://www.nytimes.com/2007/06/08/us/politics/08gays.html

26. http://www.pbs.org/moyers/journal/blog/speech/

27. http://www.nysun.com/opinion/would-goldwater-leave/30647/

28. http://www.politifact.com/truth-o-meter/statements/2008/jan/11/mike-huckabee/even-the-gipper/

29. "Reagan vs. the New Right," Jonathan Alter, *Newsweek*, September 18, 1983.

30. "Reagan Loyalists Are Wondering About Their Champion's Loyalty," Hedrick Smith, *New York Times*, November 20, 1980.

31. http://mediamatters.org/mmtv/200910220038

32. http://www.politico.com/news/stories/1209/30393.html

33. http://www.rightprinciples.com/rino1.html

34. http://tpmdc.talkingpointsmemo.com/2009/03/perkins-at-this-rate-gop-will-become-big-empty-tent.php

35. Interview with the author, 10/30/09.

36. Interview with the author, 10/20/09.

37. http://videocafe.crooksandliars.com/node/31259/print

38. http://www.worldcantwait.net/index.php?option=com_content&view=article&id=5330:obama-fact-sheet&catid=117:homepage&Itemid=289

39. Ibid.

40. http://www.warcriminalswatch.org/images/stories/pdfs/obamatorture%2017x22-wcw.pdf

41. http://dyn.politico.com/printstory.cfm?uuid=9DBDD517-18FE-70B2-A820B7CD206837AC

42. http://dyn.politico.com/printstory.cfm?uuid=9DBDD517-18FE-70B2-A820B7CD206837AC

43. http://seminal.firedoglake.com/diary/19581

44. http://www.cbsnews.com/stories/2008/12/01/politics/main4641170.shtml?source=related_story

45. http://thehill.com/blogs/blog-briefing-room/news/61611-frank-obama-wrong-to-be-post-partisan

46. http://online.wsj.com/article/SB12349165916i904365.html

47. http://seattletimes.nwsource.com/html/localnews/2002981541_sheehan09.html

48. http://www.washingtonexaminer.com/opinion/blogs/beltway-confidential/Cindy-Sheehan-heads-to-the-Vineyard-wants-anti-war-demonstrators-to-emulate-health-care-protesters-will-anyone-cover-the-story-53406107.html

49. http://www.csmonitor.com/World/Europe/2009/1210/p06s01-woeu.html

50. http://www.sj-r.com/opinions/x124603932/Ted-Rall-It-s-increasingly-evident-that-Obama-should-resign

51. http://politicalticker.blogs.cnn.com/2009/09/30/moveon-org-targets-democrats-on-public-option/

52. http://www.actblue.com/page/hitthebluedogs

53. http://voices.washingtonpost.com/ezra-klein/2009/12/joe_lieberman_lets_not_make_a.html

54. http://www.nextbookpress.com/news-and-politics/22857/liebermans-betrayal/

55. http://www.ssa.gov/history/tally.html

56. http://www.socialsecurity.gov/history/tally65.html

57. http://www.ssa.gov/history/tally1996.html

58. http://www.gallup.com/poll/123491/Approval-Congress-Falls-21-Driven-Democrats.aspx

59. http://www.gallup.com/poll/124094/Majority-Say-Obama-Policies-Mostly-Liberal.aspx

60. http://www.nationaljournal.com/njmagazine/cr_20091205_2246.php

The Big Lie: Birthers and Truthers

1. http://washingtonindependent.com/51736/rep-mike-castle-fends-off-the-birthers

2. http://www.boston.com/news/nation/articles/2008/01/26/obama_fighting_false_e_mail_rumors_in_south_carolina/

3. http://washingtonindependent.com/63817/poll-one-third-of-tennesseans-think-obama-is-muslim-or-foreign-born

4. http://pumaparty.com/vb/puma-talking-points-media-relations/18349-write-your-local-areas-newspapers-ask-if-obama-legal.html

5. http://www.factcheck.org/elections-2008/born_in_the_usa.html

6. http://pumaparty.com/forum/viewtopic.php?f=4&t=185&p=924

7. http://wwwimage.cbsnews.com/htdocs/pdf/complete_report/CBS_Report.pdf

8. Interview with the author, 12/30/09.

9. Interview with the author, 12/9/09.

10. http://www.adl.org/special_reports/rage-grows-in-America/birther-movement.asp

11. http://www.thedailybeast.com/blogs-and-stories/2009-07-30/queen-of-the-birthers/

12. http://www.wnd.com/index.php?pageId=94377

13. http://www.thedailybeast.com/blogs-and-stories/2009-07-30/queen-of-the-birthers/

14. http://drorly.blogspot.com/2009/01/what-should-be-done.html

15. http://www.salon.com/politics/war_room/feature/2009/07/22/dobbs/

16. http://thinkprogress.org/2009/06/23/gop-birther-bill/

17. http://www.washingtonmonthly.com/archives/individual/2009_03/017108.php

18. http://www.orlytaitz.com

19. http://www.washingtonpost.com/wp-dyn/content/article/2009/10/05/AR2009100503819_pf.html

20. http://www.politico.com/blogs/glennthrush/0709/58_of_GOP_not_suredont_beleive_Obama_born_in_US.html?showall

21. http://www.scrippsnews.com/911poll

22. http://97.74.65.51/readArticle.aspx?ARTID=10051

23. http://www.youtube.com/watch?v=k3wxkvsQvtQ&eurl=

24. http://reason.com/blog/2007/06/19/the-awful-truth-about-9-11

25. http://archives.cnn.com/2001/US/12/13/tape.transcript/

26. http://latimesblogs.latimes.com/washington/2009/09/obama-charlie-sheen-911.html

The Hatriots: Armed and Dangerous

1. http://www.nytimes.com/2009/12/06/us/06threat.html

2. http://oathkeepers.org/oath/2009/03/03/declaration-of-orders-we-will-not-obey/

3. http://www.splcenter.org/intel/intelreport/article.jsp?aid=1092

4. http://www.splcenter.org/intel/intelreport/article.jsp?aid=1027

5. http://www.splcenter.org/news/item.jsp?aid=392

6. http://www.threepercenter.org/page.php?al=about

7. http://www.theamericanresistancemovement.com/forums.php?a=vtopic&t=27

8. http://sipseystreetirregulars.blogspot.com/search?updated-max=2009-12-05T11%3A43%3A00-08%3A00&max-results=7

9. http://sipseystreetirregulars.blogspot.com/search?updated-max=2009-12-15T09%3A07%3A00-08%3A00&max-results=7

10. http://www.nytimes.com/2009/04/18/us/politics/18texas.html

11. http://www.huffingtonpost.com/2009/04/16/glenn-beck-secession-or-s_n_187779.html

12. http://www.huffingtonpost.com/2009/04/16/glenn-beck-secession-or-s_n_187779.html

13. http://www.washingtontimes.com/news/2009/aug/21/inside-the-beltway-68484451/

14. http://www.rightwingwatch.org/content/dobsons-lament-obama-no-reagan

15. http://www.americanthinker.com/2009/06/after_obama_fails.html

16. http://www.thedailybeast.com/blogs-and-stories/2009-11-07/stopping-the-next-mcveigh/full/

17. http://littlegreenfootballs.com/article/34899_Hot_Air_Comments_of_the_Day

18. http://littlegreenfootballs.com/article/35021_Hot_Air_Comments_of_the_Day

19. http://www.legis.ga.gov/legis/2009_10/fulltext/sr632.htm

20. http://blogs.ajc.com/jay-bookman-blog/2009/04/16/georgia-senate-threatens-dismantling-of-usa/

21. http://dixienet.org/New%20Site/index.shtml

22. Overstreet, *The Strange Tactics of Extremism,* p. 218.

23. http://www.historylink.org/index.cfm?DisplayPage=output.cfm&file_id=1464

24. http://www.columbiatribune.com/news/2009/aug/06/minuteman-outlasted-notoriety-died-with-regrets/

25. *American Jewish Year Book,* 1967.

26. http://www.textfiles.com/conspiracy/walker.txt

27. http://select.nytimes.com/gst/abstract.html?res=F50B1FFE3F5A167493CBA9178CD85F428785F9

28. "Eisenhower Says Officers Should Stay Out of Politics," *New York Times,* November 24, 1961, p. 1.

29. http://www.pbs.org/wgbh/amex/presidents/35_kennedy/psources/ps_conspir.html

30. http://www.adl.org/Learn/Ext_US/SCM.asp?LEARN_Cat=Extremism&LEARN_SubCat=Extremism_in_America&xpicked=4&item=sov

31. http://www.splcenter.org/news/item.jsp?aid=383

32. Hewitt, *Political Violence and Terrorism in Modern America,* pp. 28–90.

33. http://online.wsj.com/article/SB10001424052748704471504574447621545728370.html

34. http://thinkprogress.org/2009/07/27/gohmert-conspiracies-alexjones/

35. Interview with the author.

36. http://www.adl.org/special_reports/rage-grows-in-America/conspiracy-theories.asp

37. http://mediamatters.org/mmtv/200908310007

38. http://mediamatters.org/blog/200909290042

39. http://www.splcenter.org/blog/2009/10/07/leave-or-else-youtube-video-warns-obama/

40. http://www.post-gazette.com/pg/09095/960750-53.stm

41. http://www.huffingtonpost.com/2009/04/27/joshua-cartwright-cop-kil_n_191929.html

42. http://www.cnn.com/2009/CRIME/06/01/kansas.doctor.killed.charges/index.html

43. http://www.cnn.com/2009/CRIME/06/11/museum.shooting.suspect.two/

44. http://www.nytimes.com/2009/12/06/us/06threat.html

45. http://www.huffingtonpost.com/geoffrey-dunn/watermellon-roll-more-rac_b_152743.html_NoPara

46. http://www.splcenter.org/news/item.jsp?aid=392

47. http://www.huffingtonpost.com/2009/08/12/officials-see-rise-in-mil_n_257128.html

Conclusion: How to Take America Back
from the Lunatic Fringe

1. http://www.independent.co.uk/life-style/were-heading-into-nut-country-president-kennedy-said-this-to-an-aide-as-he-began-his-fatal-visit-to-texas-thirty-years-ago-here-peter-pringle-evokes-dallas-as-it-was-then-a-hostile-place-which-cared-very-little-for-the-dream-that-died-there-1505387.html

2. http://avalon.law.yale.edu/18th_century/washing.asp

INDEX